GUILT-FREE
FRYING

Guilt-Free Frying

Barry Bluestein
and Kevin Morrissey

H P Books

HPBooks
Published by The Berkley Publishing Group
A division of Penguin Putnam Inc.
375 Hudson Street
New York, New York 10014

Book design by Richard Oriolo

FIRST EDITION: October 1999

Published simultaneously in Canada.

The Penguin Putnam Inc. World Wide Web site address is
http://www.penguinputnam.com

Library of Congress Cataloging-in-Publication Data

Bluestein, Barry.
    Guilt-free frying / Barry Bluestein and Kevin Morrissey. — 1st
  ed.
        p.   cm.
    ISBN 1-55788-318-1
    1. Frying.   2. Low-fat diet Recipes.   I. Morrissey, Kevin.
  II. Title.
  TX689.B58   1999
  641.7'7—dc2l   99–35635
                                                          CIP

Printed in the United States of America

10 9 8 7 6 5 4 3 2

For Deborah Donevan Hendricks, Jim Hendricks,
and in memory of Beauregard Jefferson Hendricks III

ACKNOWLEDGMENTS

We're grateful to John Duff for his vision, Jeanette Egan for her diligence, and to everyone else at Penguin Putnam Inc. who helped birth this book, including Charles Björklund, Kristen Green, Lisa Miscione, Barbara O'Shea, Tess Bresnan, and Miguel Santana. Thanks to Grant Kessler for his photography, to Mark Sterwald of the Mirro Company for his marvelous baking sheets, and to Lisa Ekus, Merrilyn Lewis, and Allison Wood at Lisa Ekus Public Relations Co. for their ongoing support.

So many others have contributed so much to our work—Tammy Blake, Ann Bloomstrand, Eleanor Bluestein, Chris Broyles, Don Houck, Judy Kern, Claudia Clark Potter, Susan Ramer, Leslie Revsin, William Rice, Martha Schueneman, Mark Stahr, and Jill Van Cleave among them. Thank you one and all.

CONTENTS

INTRODUCTION

"I usually avoid fried foods these days," a slim urban dweller was recently overheard to say, "but you've got to try the catfish at this new soul food restaurant!"

"I never eat anything fried anymore," her companion said. "But hush puppies don't count, do they?"

To fry or not to fry often seems a moot point these days, since most cooks think they know what the answer is—or at least what it should be. Much like the double cheeseburger, hollandaise sauce, and pecan pie heaped with whipped cream, fried foods are fast being relegated to the realm of the occasional indulgence, if not banished completely from our increasingly health-conscious diets.

And then there's the mess. Even if we convince ourselves that not all of the fat grams from the buckets of oil in which frying is typically done will actually make their way into the food, the thought of cleaning up the greasy film that deep-frying invariably leaves on all surfaces in the near vicinity is enough to deter lots of folks. Not to mention the fact that there's something a little bit frightening about tending a skillet from which blobs of oil heated to 365F (185C) are spattering—frying a piece or two at a time—and trying to keep the oil hot enough to continue while the cooked pieces become limp and lukewarm.

Nonetheless, we still dream about the distinctive pleasure of sinking our teeth into favorite fried foods. We fear the fat and we shy away from the process, but we do love the end results. From onion rings to spring rolls to fritters, doughnuts to potato pancakes and even to fried chicken, we all have mouthwatering memories. One friend, a svelte New Yorker who probably hasn't picked up a

French fry in years, recently spoke with passion about experiencing "deep-fry deprivation."

No Muss, No Fuss "Fried" Food

What most modern cooks don't realize in their fervor to banish fat from the dining table and mess from the kitchen is that enjoying "fried" foods is not an all-or-nothing proposition. Taking our friend's words about deep-fry deprivation as a challenge to be met, we set out on a culinary quest. Doing away with the muss, the fuss, and the fat while retaining the texture and taste of fried foods, from the first heavenly crunch of the coating to the last lick of the fingers, became our obsession. Lean and clean was our goal as we battered and breaded incessantly, baked and griddled without pause, and sautéed and stir-fried the days away—always posing three critical queries before a recipe made the cut: Does it look like fried? Does it crunch like fried? Does it taste like fried?

For inspiration, we closed our eyes and conjured up visions of fried foods we had enjoyed over the years and around the country. We reveled in recollections of the crisp fried clams dispensed by many a ramshackle New England seafood shack, the crusty crab cakes served up in the old food court in Baltimore or across the bay on the Eastern Shore, and the succulent conch fritters of the Florida Keys.

Kevin recalled his first loving taste of catfish and hush puppies as a child, in an antebellum mansion outside Nashville, and an initial encounter a decade or so later with the unique country cooking phenomenon known as chicken-fried steak, savored at Don's Eat and Barbecue in rural mid-Missouri.

Barry countered with flashbacks of the world's best doughnuts, which flew off the shelves of a Houston truck stop by 7:00 every morning, an addictive western omelet sandwich that was the specialty of an unlikely greasy spoon nestled amid the glass and steel towers of Sunset Boulevard in Hollywood, and the awesome buttermilk-marinated, cayenne-infused Southern fried chicken made by the mother of a colleague when he worked at Motown.

Together, we drooled in anticipation of re-creating the oyster po'boys and beignets of old French Quarter haunts, the spicy fried crabs that transcend the plastic tablecloths and slightly garish decor of a favorite Seattle hole in the wall, and the diminutive smelts that devotees fry up fresh on the Lake Michigan shore back home in Chicago.

Through trial and error, we discovered the best crumbs for the crunchiest of coatings, the most suitable pans, and the most workable techniques. In many of our recipes we hot-oven bake, which in conjunction with just the right breading preparation gives a crisp outer shell and a golden brown hue virtually indistinguishable from that of deep-frying. We take full advantage of new nonstick surfaces that let us dry-fry and griddle with only an occasional spritz of olive or canola oil for flavor, and stir-fry in stock instead of a sea of peanut oil.

In the pages that follow, we offer our renditions of a wide range of fried treats that weigh in with but a fraction of the fat of the original versions. With these recipes, you can "fry" to your heart's delight with no guilt. You can savor the sizzle while sparing the spatter. And you can serve it all up piping hot to a houseful of friends with no need to stand guard by a bubbling cauldron.

TECHNIQUES

Hot-Oven Baking

The right combination of dredging, dipping, and breading before baking in a very hot oven (at temperatures of 400 to 500F; 205 to 260C) gives many foods the same crisp outside coating as would deep-frying. Often we call for preheating a baking sheet along with the oven. A mist of cooking spray when you then put the food down on the hot sheet will sear the food much as would submerging it in a skillet of hot oil. When you put the chicken breasts we prepare in the manner of Buffalo wings down on a hot baking sheet, bone side up, for example, the crusty, browned patches usually associated with pan-frying form on the surface, even though the skin has been removed.

The secret to the success of hot-oven baking is in the crumb. In deep-frying, foods are typically either battered in a flour and liquid mixture or dredged in seasoned flour or a light crumb, both of which methods produce a distinctively hefty, granular texture when the food hits hot oil. Our recipes use two or three layers of ingredients that work together to closely replicate the texture of frying when the food is baked in a very hot oven.

In most of these recipes, you first dip (or marinate) food in a liquid, often buttermilk or egg white, which will help the coating to stick, taking care to cover all crevices thoroughly. You then coat well with a crumb or a mixture of crumbs, including breadcrumbs, cracker crumbs, wheat germ, cornmeal, and cookie crumbs for sweets. In some cases, when the liquid alone would not by itself be sufficient to hold the crumb, the food is first dredged lightly in flour. Porous doughnuts do not require dredging before dipping; skinless chicken breasts do.

In addition to the obvious benefits of eliminating the fat and the mess associated with deep-frying in oil, hot-oven baking allows for more creative breading. In some dishes, we add such novel touches to the crumbs as fresh herbs or sun-dried tomatoes, which would burn in hot oil.

Dry-Frying, Griddling, and Stir-Frying

The latest generation of nonstick coatings is truly remarkable and virtually eliminates the need for adding fat. We discovered some time ago how easy it is to sweat vegetables, cooking them in their own moisture in lieu of automatically reaching for a bottle of oil every time you sauté. In developing our dry-frying repertoire, we came to appreciate the true potential for these surfaces even more.

Crepes cook beautifully when you pour the batter into a preheated, ungreased nonstick pan, and the crepe will actually rise off the pan enough to allow you to slide a spatula underneath, effortlessly, just at the time the crepe is perfectly cooked and lightly browned. When griddling such dishes as crawfish cakes and panini, you can spritz the food with oil before placing it on the preheated nonstick surface, just to aid browning and add a little flavor, without the need for excessive greasing to prevent sticking.

When you stir-fry in a nonstick pan or a well-seasoned wok, you can easily skip the usual dose of oil. In typical stir-frying, the vegetables are cooked in oil and removed, the oil is reheated, and then the meat or seafood is cooked in the oil before sauce is added and the vegetables are returned to the pan.

We prepare our stir-fries by cooking the vegetables in a little broth or water and the meat or seafood in its marinade, which will work just fine as long as you keep the food in constant motion to prevent burning or overcooking. With a wooden spatula or paddle in each hand, move the food up from the bottom of the pan, tossing and turning it over so that it will cook evenly. When you add the sauce, pour it in slowly all around the pan and then toss the meat and vegetables quickly, so that the sauce will not thicken too quickly from the high heat.

EQUIPMENT

Baking Sheets: Choose nonstick baking sheets that are made from heavy-gauge metal that will withstand high oven temperatures without warping. In cookware lingo, the lower the gauge, the heavier the pan. Look for 4- or 6-gauge baking sheets and for such descriptive phrases as "professional," "extra-thick," and "reinforced rim." Although we normally love the sheets made with double layers of metal and a cushion of air in between, they won't work for hot-oven baking—the insulation that makes it virtually impossible to burn goods baked on this type of sheet will prevent these foods from becoming as crisp and crusty as desired. If at all possible, visit a restaurant supply store, which will have a broader range of heavy-duty cookware at more reasonable prices than those at department stores and kitchenware stores. Choose sheets measuring at least 18 × 13 inches.

Doughnut Cutters: These handy gadgets, usually measuring about 2¾ inches across, have both an outer cutter much like a biscuit or cookie cutter and an inner cutter (which will neatly separate the dough for the hole, leaving a perfectly shaped doughnut). Unfortunately, they're somewhat scarcer these days than when our grandmothers were whipping up doughnuts routinely—we're using someone's grandma's cutter, which we found in a junk shop. You can also improvise by cutting the dough circles out with a 3-inch-diameter biscuit cutter, cookie cutter, or glass. Use any 1-inch circular object to cut out the hole.

Meat Pounders or Meat Tenderizers: To pound steak or other meat sufficiently thin for a chicken-fried, or country-fried, preparation, you'll need a broad, flat meat pounder; a meat tenderizer, which resembles a hammer with a waffled surface; or a sturdy rubber mallet (which is what we use).

Mini Food Processors or Mini Blender Jars: The handiest appliances for easily chopping crackers, wafers, and the like to a fine crumb are 2-cup-capacity mini food processors or the 1-cup jar attachments that come with many blenders. Both are so terrific for chopping herbs and small quantities of veggies that we use ours constantly.

Oven Mitts: Before you make a single recipe, be sure you have a pair of heavy, well-insulated oven mitts on hand. Baking sheets emerging from a 500F (260C) oven are far too hot to be picked up with a single thickness of kitchen towel or one of those cute little pot holders from a souvenir shop.

Pans: Look for pans made from 8-gauge metal (which is at least $\frac{1}{16}$ inch thick) or heavier (the lower the gauge, the better), which will withstand preheating over high heat without warping. Grasp the pan along the edge opposite the handle and see if it tilts downward from the weight of the handle. If it does, keep looking; the heft should be in the pan, not the handle. Pans with a nonstick coating labeled "Silverstone with ScratchGuard" are so durable and scratch-resistant that you can use whisks and other metal utensils without worrying about marring the pan's surface. Cast-iron pans also work well since they are heavy and, once seasoned, have an interior surface that is naturally nonstick. Skillets with a 7- or 8-inch diameter are usually considered small; 9- and 10-inch skillets, medium; and those with a 12-inch diameter or greater, large. Stir-fry pans and woks usually measure about 12 inches across the top. We use a two-handled 20 × 11-inch griddle that fits over 2 burners, but you could use one of the round cast-iron griddles that fit over a single burner.

Stir-fry pans have flat bottoms that work on all types of cooktops, whereas curved-bottom woks can't be used on some, such as the smooth-surface electric varieties. Few woks have nonstick coatings, but their interiors become naturally nonstick once seasoned, much like cast iron. To season a wok, preheat it over high heat, swirl in about a tablespoon of oil to coat, and place it in a preheated 350F (175C) oven for 30 minutes, swirling the oil every 10 minutes. Just as you would a cast-iron pan, wipe the wok clean rather than scrub it.

Plastic Bags: For marinating, we often use heavy-duty, self-sealing freezer storage bags, which work well and make for easy cleanup. Mix the ingredients for the marinade well in the bag, add the food to be marinated, press the air out, seal, and "massage" the marinade into the food. Lighter storage bags can be used for mixing food with a crumb mixture or dredging with flour.

Spatulas and Tongs: Since baking sheets get very hot in high temperature ovens, spatulas that can withstand the heat are in order. Metal spatulas hold up well, but beware of scratching if you use them with baking sheets or pans that do not have a scratch-resistant coating. The large spring-hinge tongs that can be found in kitchenware stores and some department stores facilitate handling pieces of chicken, ribs, and other larger food items. Choose the rustproof, stainless steel kind.

Spice or Coffee Grinders: Either of these small appliances will grind seeds and other coarse ingredients for seasoning blends much more finely than will a food processor, even a mini food processor.

INGREDIENTS

Meat, poultry, shellfish, and fish are generally specified by weight in ingredient lists. Produce is called for by cup measurement when the chopped, sliced, or otherwise prepped measure is derived from less than a whole raw ingredient (e.g., ¼ cup chopped bell pepper is derived from less than one bell pepper) or when a very precise prepped measure is needed (e.g., 2 tablespoons of a mixture of shredded carrot and thinly sliced green onion are to be placed in the center of each wonton skin or pastry square). Otherwise, we call for a specific number of whole raw ingredients (e.g., 2 plum tomatoes or 1 red potato), specifying desired weight in the case of ingredients that can vary greatly in size or for larger quantities.

Beans: In several recipes, you can use either cooked dried beans or canned beans. In planning, know that 1 cup of dried beans will yield 3 cups of cooked beans and that a 15-ounce can of beans contains about 1½ cups cooked beans. If you go the canned route, select an organic brand, which will contain no salt and very little fat, and be sure to rinse and drain the beans thoroughly.

Beef

- Lean, thin flank steak is suited to stir-fries because it takes well to marinating and to quick cooking at high temperatures.

- Once well trimmed, sirloin is leaner than flank steak. It's also a more versatile cut of meat. Flank steak should be served on the rare side, whereas sirloin is good even when cooked until more well done.

- The tip round steak used for chicken-fried preparation is also quite lean. Because the steak is pounded so thin in this preparation, you can use lower-grade, lower-fat "select" meat rather than opting for prime or choice.

- When a recipe calls for ground beef, select a lean cut, such as sirloin. Have your butcher trim and grind the meat, or grind it at home as directed on page 29.

Black Pepper: Specific measures of ground black pepper are given in most recipes to facilitate the calculation of nutritional values. However, we recommend that you use freshly ground pepper—you can add an extra grind or two to taste without any significant addition of fat or calories.

Breadcrumbs: Although our nutritional counts are based on the use of prepared breadcrumbs, you can make your own in a food processor. Not only will the crumbs taste fresher, they will likely be a bit lower in fat. Two 1-ounce slices of bread will yield about ½ cup of breadcrumbs. See the recipes on page 22 for French Bread you can use to make French Breadcrumbs, and on page 23 for Italian-Style Breadcrumbs that can be made from homemade French bread or from store-bought French or Italian bread.

Broth: Homemade broths are quite a bit richer and tastier than the commercial varieties, and we heartily recommend you make your own when time allows and store them in 1- and 2-cup portions in the freezer. See the recipes on pages 19–21 for homemade chicken broth, vegetable broth (quite a bit better than prepared, as we first roast the vegetables), and beef broth. If you use commercial broths, select the fat-free varieties.

Butter: We use small amounts of butter in our recipes. Choose unsalted butter. Substitute margarine if you prefer.

Buttermilk: We make liberal use of thick, rich buttermilk in our recipes. It can tenderize as a marinade and replaces the texture of the fatty layer that is removed from chicken with the skin. Contrary to the common misconception, buttermilk is a clotted skim or low-fat milk product that contains no butter. In addition to the cartons in your supermarket's dairy case, buttermilk comes in powdered form, allowing you to use just a little bit at a time. You can make your own by putting 1 tablespoon distilled white vinegar in a 1-cup measuring cup, adding enough 1 percent milk to make 1 cup, and letting the mixture sit at room temperature for about 10 minutes. In a pinch, substitute plain nonfat yogurt for buttermilk.

Buttermilk Baking Mix: There are several brands available; the most popular is Bisquick. You can use the reduced-fat variety, as we do.

Calamari: Always buy calamari, aka squid, that has been cleaned. You can substitute the scarce, but slightly tenderer, cuttlefish should you find some.

Capers: We generally prefer the larger and more flavorful Italian capers to the little nonpareils. Be sure to rinse off the brine before adding them to a recipe. Capers also come packed in salt; rinse them well, then pat them dry, if you use this variety.

Catfish: Once a Southern delicacy, catfish has become quite common in most regions now that it is farm-raised. Where you can't get it fresh, you can certainly find it frozen.

Cheese

- When we call for *queso*, a mild Mexican cheese, buy *queso fresco* (fresh) rather than aged, which has quite a bit more fat.

- Any mild white cheese can be substituted for Mexican *asadero* or Chihuahua cheese if you can't find it.

- We've found that robust blue cheese is the base for very good sauces and dips. It is so flavorful that a little goes a long way, and it mixes well with such low-fat ingredients as buttermilk.

- When we call for ricotta cheese, choose skim milk ricotta.

- Look for farmer cheese in your supermarket dairy case. If you want to substitute cottage cheese, put it into a sieve that has been lined with a damp coffee filter, then place the sieve over a bowl. Refrigerate it overnight to allow the whey to drain from the cheese.

- In many instances, nonfat feta cheese can be substituted for goat cheese, although it will give a somewhat drier, more crumbly consistency.

- Although we have calculated nutritional information based on the use of small quantities of full-fat cheese unless otherwise specified (as in the case of skim milk ricotta), feel free to substitute readily identifiable lower-fat alternatives, such as reduced-fat for full-fat Swiss cheese.

- On those rare occasions when we call for a sprinkle of Parmesan cheese, use freshly grated cheese rather than the tasteless dried variety.

Chicken: Many of our poultry recipes use chicken breasts; a few that demand a richer, heartier meat use thighs or legs. Nutritional counts for whole chicken are based upon an equal distribution of the leaner white meat and fattier dark meat. Other than in the case of chicken wing appetizers, we remove skin. As you plan your indulgences, bear in mind that breast meat has only about a third the fat of dark meat. (When you compare skinless breast meat against a thigh with skin, the ratio is more like 10:1.) Whatever part of the chicken you opt for, it will taste better if you start with a free-range bird.

Chinese Broccoli: We much prefer this robust, flavorful vegetable to plain old broccoli, especially in stir-fries. If your market doesn't stock it, try the equally pungent broccoli rabe, also called rapini.

Clams: We usually use Atlantic cherrystones because they are so easy to find, but you could easily substitute littlenecks or any of the Pacific varieties. Razor clams, a soft-shell variety, are particularly good fried. See page 112 for shucking directions.

Coconut Milk: Choose "light" coconut milk, which packs only a fraction of the fat grams of coconut milk or the even richer coconut cream.

Conch: We recommend you buy this abalone-like Caribbean mollusk canned, because it is ready to use with no further tenderization needed. Look in Asian, Caribbean, or Italian groceries if you can't find conch in your supermarket.

Cornmeal: For each recipe that uses a cornmeal crumb, we've selected the type we think works best from the range of cornmeals, which include coarse-ground Italian cornmeal (often called polenta), the finer-grain domestic variety, and yellow and white cornmeal. In one recipe we call for a crumb of blue corn chips, since blue cornmeal can be a bit difficult to find in some areas—if you can find it, by all means use it.

Crab

- Crabmeat is readily available at supermarket fish counters. If you use a lot, you may want to consider buying it frozen by the pound, as we do from our local Asian market.

- In recipes that call for whole crab, we prefer the larger and meatier Dungeness crabs from the West Coast to Eastern blue crabs. They're sold frozen in gourmet and Asian markets, and fresh in some fish markets.

- Soft-shell crab recipes are best made from spring to early fall, when soft-shells (Atlantic and Gulf blue crabs that have shed their hard shells) are available fresh. Farm-raised soft-shells can be found all year long in the freezers of many supermarkets.

Crawfish: These tasty little bayou crustaceans are now farm-raised and widely available in most of the country. Many supermarkets sell both crawfish in their shells and shelled crawfish meat.

Eggs: In many recipes, we dip food into lightly beaten egg white to help the crumbs adhere. When we make egg dishes, we usually use a mixture of whole egg and egg white so as to provide fewer fat grams than would the use of whole egg alone. In either type of recipe, if you are not concerned with the added fat and cholesterol, you can substitute 1 whole egg for every 2 egg whites. In most instances, you could also substitute ¼ cup liquid egg substitute for every 2 egg whites.

Egg Roll Wrappers: Also called egg roll skins, these can be found frozen or refrigerated in Asian markets and most supermarkets. You can also use *lumpia,* which are Philippine egg roll skins.

Extracts: Always choose pure extracts rather than imitation.

Frogs' Legs: Frogs' legs are available frozen in most parts of the country. They can be found fresh during spring and summer in some gourmet markets. Take care not to overcook the legs, which will toughen them.

Garlic Powder and Onion Powder: Although we normally pass these seasonings by in favor of fresh garlic and onion, we do use them in frying recipes. Both powders can add flavor to a breading without burning (as would their fresh counterparts).

Ginger: Do not substitute ground ginger for wonderfully aromatic and readily available fresh gingerroot. Look for wrinkle-free young ginger, which is free of any trace of the bitterness that can taint aging ginger.

Green Tomatoes: Firmer and less sweet than red tomatoes, green tomatoes take well to such savory preparations as frying. They are not some exotic species, just tomatoes that have not been allowed to ripen on the vine long enough to turn red. Green tomatoes are particularly prevalent in summer and fall.

Herbs: We much prefer to use fresh herbs and call for them liberally, but you can substitute dried herbs in a pinch in most cases; use about a third of the volume of fresh herb specified.

Hot Sauces: Much to the delight of lovers of things hot and spicy, there are literally dozens of hot sauces on the market, most of them made from red chile peppers. The Tabasco brand has recently introduced a hot green pepper sauce that we find both milder and more complex than its popular red sauce.

Masa Harina: We often use this corn flour, the staple ingredient of such classic Mexican dishes as tamales and tortillas, which has a much finer texture than cornmeal. Look in either the baking or the Latin section of your supermarket.

Monkfish: A delicacy in much of the world, the eminently unattractive monkfish, the tail meat of which is the only edible portion, has recently come to be appreciated in the United States. Beneath the homely exterior lies firm, delicate, faintly sweet fish.

Oil: We eschew the liberal dose of oil typically associated with frying, but do use small amounts to lightly coat pans and spray food with oil to promote browning. Although you can use a commercial cooking spray, we highly recommend the modest investment in an oil mister, available from kitchenware stores and department stores. These polished steel cylinders are fitted with a pump that forces the oil up and out, dispensing pure oil without the alcohol and propellants contained in the commercial products.

Oysters: East Coast bluepoints are the most common, but feel free to mix and match a range of types, including Atlantic Malpeques and Wellfleets, Pacific oysters, Olympia oysters from Washington state, and French belons, which are now farm-raised in the United States. To shuck oysters, follow the directions on page 112.

Paprika: Unless we specifically call for "hot" paprika, use the milder, more common sweet paprika. In either case, buy imported Hungarian paprika, which is now in just about every supermarket.

Plantains: A Latin American relative of the banana used more as a starch, plantains are now common in urban supermarkets. They turn from green to yellow to black and sweeten slightly as they ripen.

Pork

- We have recently rediscovered pork tenderloin, a tasty cut that is surprisingly low in fat and that comes trimmed in pieces usually weighing less than a pound.
- Grind your own pork tenderloin (see page 29 for directions) for recipes that call for ground pork, or have your butcher grind it for you. Preground pork can contain quite a bit of fat.
- For recipes more suited to center-cut pork chops, have your butcher trim off the outer layer of fat.
- For pork chop sandwiches or country-fried preparation, choose boneless top loin chops.
- When ribs are in order, choose baby back pork loin ribs, which have less than half the fat of spareribs, and are more tender. Have the butcher cut the slab in half horizontally for portions that are easier to eat and satisfying without being overindulgent.

Potatoes: Use firm, dry baking potatoes for chips and fries. For thicker-cut sliced potato recipes, use red potatoes, which brown quite nicely. For the best mashed potatoes, there's only one choice, Yukon Gold potatoes.

Quail: Diminutive quail are low in fat. Look for them in the freezers of gourmet markets or Asian markets. They can sometimes be ordered fresh from butcher shops. Hot-oven baking seals in juices and prevents them from drying out.

Rabbit: Rabbit is almost all white meat, relatively low in saturated fat and calories, and high in mineral content. Most butcher shops and many supermarkets now stock rabbit, which is sold both fresh and frozen.

Rice

- The most common rice used to make risottos and risotto cakes is arborio, a starchy, short-grain Italian rice. If you develop a taste for risotto dishes and have access to an importer of finer Italian products, try either the superb Vialone Nano rice or Carnaroli rice.

- Rich, nutty, slightly chewy wild rice is sold in many better supermarkets and in gourmet stores. It's becoming more readily available as commercial cultivation augments its small natural growth in the upper Midwest. Wild rice can be gritty, and should first be rinsed.

- Look for nutty brown basmati rice in supermarkets or Middle Eastern markets. It is a particularly aromatic species of rice.

Roasted Peppers: In cooked dishes that call for roasted sweet bell pepper, we often opt for the preroasted variety that comes in a jar and can be found in the Italian section of many supermarkets. To roast your own, broil cored and seeded bell pepper halves in the broiler, cut side down, for about 5 minutes, until charred. Cool them in a plastic storage bag and then rub the skins off.

Salt Cod: Firm and flavorful salt-preserved cod can be found in Italian, Caribbean, and African markets. It is reconstituted by soaking it in water for 12 to 36 hours. It retains a salty taste even though much of the sodium content is flushed from the fish while it soaks.

Scallops: We call for sea scallops in our recipes because the diminutive bay scallops are very difficult to bread. Besides, sea scallops are consistently good, whereas highly seasonal bay scallops can vary greatly in quality.

Seasoning Blends: While you can easily buy commercially prepared versions of the seasoning blends we call for in our recipes, you can make your own in a matter of minutes. We like the freshness and added robustness of homemade seasonings (which should be stored in sealed, opaque containers to lengthen shelf life). See the recipes on pages 23–28.

Shrimp

- Rock shrimp, a crustacean found in the Atlantic Ocean and Gulf of Mexico, has firm, sweet meat much like that of a lobster. If you can't find it, substitute an equal amount of medium shrimp.

- Freshwater prawns, for which colossal shrimp can be substituted, are farm-raised in many landlocked areas of the country.

- Miniature shrimp, or salad shrimp, are available both fresh and canned. Inhabitants of the Pacific Northwest can use the tiny, local cold-water shrimp instead.

Smelts: These succulent little fish, with bones so delicate they can be eaten whole, are available fresh in some regions (they're called rainbow smelts in the East, candlefish on the West Coast) from fall through spring. Elsewhere, they can often be found flash-frozen.

Snapper: An attractive fish perfectly suited to presentation whole, snapper is available all year. Select red snapper, which is smaller and somewhat sweeter than other varieties. It has big, easily removed bones.

Sprouts: Always cook sprouts, just as you would meat or fish; they have been identified as a source of bacterial contamination in their raw state.

Tilapia: A farm-raised fish that has a mild, subtly sweet flavor, firm white flesh, and very little fat—a combination that undoubtedly accounts for its growing popularity.

Trout: Use either steelhead or sea trout, both of which are much larger and firmer textured than the smaller brook trout. Steelhead trout is a salmon-colored subspecies of rainbow trout.

Turkey

- Use turkey breast tenderloin, which has less fat than any other cut of poultry.

- Grind your own turkey breast tenderloin—or have your butcher grind it for you—rather than opting for preground turkey, which can contain fat and skin. Follow the directions on page 29 for grinding meat.

- When a recipe calls for smoked turkey breast, buy a real smoked breast on the bone instead of settling for a chunk of pressed turkey.

Veal: Veal leg cutlets are the leanest cut of veal, the cut that is pounded thin for scallopine. We rather like the slightly gamy taste of free-range veal, which is the only type that many of your guests will eat.

Whole-Wheat Flour and Wheat Germ: We use whole-wheat flour in our heartier doughnuts and wheat germ to provide a distinctive crumb. Both have poor shelf life. Buy them in small quantities and store them in the refrigerator.

Wonton Skins: Look in your supermarket freezer case for both round and square wonton skins, also called dumpling skins.

THE BASICS

CHICKEN BROTH

MAKES ABOUT 8 CUPS

4 pounds chicken bones (with meat scraps)

2 carrots, cut into chunks

1 large yellow onion, cut into chunks

2 stalks celery, cut into chunks

4 quarts water

1 teaspoon salt

1 bay leaf

Combine the chicken bones, carrots, onion, celery, water, salt, and bay leaf in a stockpot. Bring to a rapid boil. Skim the surface and reduce the heat to low. Skimming periodically, simmer, uncovered, until the bones begin to fall apart, about 3 hours.

Remove and discard the bones, vegetables, and bay leaf. Strain the broth into a large bowl and refrigerate for 2 to 3 hours.

Scrape off the layer of fat that rises to the top of the broth.

OUR SELECTION OF guilt-free fried dishes includes the following basics:

Chicken Broth

Vegetable Broth

Beef Broth

French Bread

Italian-Style Breadcrumbs

Adobo Seasoning

Cajun Seasoning

Chili Powder

Chinese Five-Spice Powder

Creole Seasoning

Curry Powder

Italian Seasoning

Jerk Seasoning

Lemon Pepper

Poultry Seasoning

Seafood Seasoning

VEGETABLE BROTH

3 tomatoes, quartered, or 6 plum tomatoes, halved

2 large yellow onions, halved

2 carrots, halved

2 stalks celery, halved

6 cloves garlic, peeled

4 bay leaves

2 sprigs fresh parsley

2 sprigs fresh thyme

12 whole black peppercorns

4 quarts water

Preheat the oven to 450F (230C).

Place the tomatoes, onions, carrots, and celery in a baking dish. Roast for 10 minutes, turn the vegetables over, and roast for 10 minutes more.

Transfer the contents of the baking dish to a stockpot. Add the garlic, bay leaves, parsley, thyme, peppercorns, and water and bring to a rapid boil. Skim the surface and reduce the heat to low. Skimming periodically, simmer, uncovered, for 2 hours.

Strain the broth into a large bowl, pressing down on the vegetables to extract as much juice as possible.

BEEF BROTH

4 pounds beef bones (with meat scraps)

3 tomatoes, quartered, or 6 plum tomatoes, halved

1 large yellow onion, quartered

1 carrot, halved

1 stalk celery, halved

4 bay leaves

1 teaspoon whole black peppercorns

½ tablespoon salt

5 quarts water

MAKES 6 TO 8 CUPS

Preheat the oven to 400F (205C).

Arrange the beef bones in a single layer in a large baking dish. Roast for 30 minutes. Turn the bones over, add the tomatoes, onion, carrot, and celery, and roast for 20 minutes more.

Transfer the contents of the baking dish to a stockpot. Add the bay leaves, peppercorns, salt, and water. Bring to a rapid boil, skim the surface, and reduce the heat to low. Skimming periodically, simmer, uncovered, for 4 hours.

Remove and discard the bones, vegetables, and bay leaves. Strain the broth into a large bowl and refrigerate it for 2 to 3 hours.

Scrape off the layer of fat that rises to the top of the broth.

FRENCH BREAD

MAKES 1 (15-INCH) LOAF

FRENCH BREADCRUMBS

For breadcrumbs, slice the loaf and let the slices sit at room temperature overnight to dry out a bit. Break the slices into chunks and finely grind them in a food processor or blender. The full loaf will make about 3¾ cups breadcrumbs.

¾ teaspoon sugar

¼ cup lukewarm water (105 to 115F; 40 to 45C)

2¼ teaspoons (1 envelope) active dry yeast

2½ cups bread flour

½ cup whole-wheat flour

½ teaspoon salt

1 cup room-temperature water

Dissolve the sugar in the lukewarm water. Stir in the yeast and set aside to proof until bubbly, about 5 minutes.

In the bowl of a food processor, combine the flours and salt. Process for 1 minute. Scrape in the yeast mixture, turn the machine on, and drizzle the room-temperature water in through the feed tube until a dough ball forms. (You may not need to use the full cup.) Continue to process until the dough ball has made 30 revolutions.

Remove the dough ball to a large glass or ceramic bowl that has been coated lightly with cooking spray. Cover it loosely with a damp towel and set aside to rise until the dough has about doubled in size and no longer springs back to the touch, about 1½ hours.

On a work surface, flatten the dough and shape it into a 15 × 10-inch rectangle, then roll it up into a 15-inch loaf. Place the loaf in a nonstick French bread pan or on a nonstick baking sheet. Re-cover with a damp towel and set aside until doubled in size, about 1 hour.

Preheat the oven to 425F (220C).

Make 3 diagonal slashes in the top of the loaf with a sharp knife. Spritz the loaf lightly with water and bake for 5 minutes. Spritz with water again and bake for about 25 minutes more, until the bread has browned and sounds hollow when tapped on the bottom. Remove it to a wire rack to cool.

ITALIAN-STYLE BREADCRUMBS

1 cup breadcrumbs from French or Italian bread (see opposite)

1 tablespoon dried basil

2 teaspoons onion powder

1 teaspoon garlic powder

½ teaspoon salt

Mix all ingredients together in a small bowl.

MAKES ABOUT 1 CUP

ADOBO SEASONING

1 tablespoon dried oregano

2 teaspoons dried thyme

2 teaspoons coarse salt

2 teaspoons ground cumin

2 teaspoons garlic powder

2 teaspoons paprika

½ tablespoon ground coriander

½ tablespoon granulated light brown sugar

1 teaspoon cayenne pepper

1 teaspoon ground cinnamon

Mix all ingredients together in a small bowl.

Seasoning Blends

MAKES ABOUT
6 TABLESPOONS

CAJUN SEASONING

MAKES ABOUT
6 TABLESPOONS

½ tablespoon finely chopped lemon zest

1 tablespoon cayenne pepper

1 tablespoon ground black pepper

1 tablespoon coarse salt

2 teaspoons dried thyme

2 teaspoons ground cumin

2 teaspoons paprika

½ tablespoon garlic powder

Set the lemon zest aside to air-dry for about 1 hour. Mix the dried zest with the remaining ingredients.

CHILI POWDER

MAKES ABOUT
6 TABLESPOONS

2 dried ancho chiles (about 1 ounce total)

½ teaspoon cumin seeds

1½ tablespoons garlic powder

1½ tablespoons dried oregano

½ tablespoon ground coriander

¼ teaspoon ground cloves

Core and seed the chiles, then tear them into small pieces. Combine the torn chiles and the cumin seeds in a spice or coffee grinder and grind finely. Add the remaining ingredients and grind to blend.

CHINESE FIVE-SPICE POWDER

12 whole star anise

3 tablespoons fennel seeds

1 tablespoon whole black peppercorns

3 tablespoons ground cinnamon

3 tablespoons ground cloves

MAKES ABOUT
6 TABLESPOONS

Combine the anise, fennel seeds, and peppercorns in a spice or coffee grinder and grind finely. Add the remaining ingredients and grind to blend.

CREOLE SEASONING

2 tablespoons ground black pepper

1 tablespoon plus 1 teaspoon dried thyme

1 tablespoon plus 1 teaspoon paprika

1 tablespoon plus 1 teaspoon cayenne pepper

1 tablespoon plus 1 teaspoon coarse salt

MAKES ABOUT
7 TABLESPOONS

Mix all ingredients together in a small bowl.

Curry Powder

MAKES ABOUT
6 TABLESPOONS

2 tablespoons ground coriander

1 tablespoon ground turmeric

1 tablespoon ground cumin

1 tablespoon celery seeds

1 teaspoon ground ginger

1 teaspoon ground cloves

¾ teaspoon ground black pepper

¾ teaspoon ground nutmeg

Mix all ingredients together in a small bowl.

Italian Seasoning

MAKES ABOUT
6 TABLESPOONS

1½ tablespoons dried thyme

1½ tablespoons dried oregano

1 tablespoon dried rosemary

½ tablespoon dried marjoram

½ tablespoon dried winter savory

1 teaspoon aniseed

1 teaspoon rubbed sage

1 teaspoon dried basil

Mix all ingredients together in a small bowl.

JERK SEASONING

1½ tablespoons ground allspice

1½ tablespoons granulated light brown sugar

½ tablespoon ground cinnamon

½ tablespoon ground black pepper

½ tablespoon dried thyme

½ tablespoon coarse salt

½ tablespoon garlic powder

½ teaspoon ground nutmeg

½ teaspoon cayenne pepper

¼ teaspoon rubbed sage

MAKES ABOUT
6 TABLESPOONS

Mix all ingredients together in a small bowl.

LEMON PEPPER

2 tablespoons plus 2 teaspoons finely chopped lemon zest
(about 2 large lemons)

2 tablespoons coarse ground black pepper

2 tablespoons coarse salt

¼ teaspoon garlic powder

¼ teaspoon onion powder

¼ teaspoon sugar

MAKES ABOUT
6 TABLESPOONS

Set the lemon zest aside to air-dry for about 1 hour. Mix the dried
zest with the remaining ingredients.

POULTRY SEASONING

2 tablespoons dried rosemary

2 tablespoons rubbed sage

1 tablespoon plus 1 teaspoon dried oregano

½ tablespoon ground ginger

½ teaspoon ground black pepper

Mix all ingredients together in a small bowl.

SEAFOOD SEASONING

3 tablespoons coarse salt

1½ tablespoons celery seed

1 tablespoon paprika

¾ teaspoon cayenne pepper

¾ teaspoon ground black pepper

½ teaspoon ground cloves

½ teaspoon ground cinnamon

¼ teaspoon ground allspice

¼ teaspoon ground ginger

¼ teaspoon ground mace

⅛ teaspoon dry mustard

Combine the salt and celery seed in a spice or coffee grinder and grind finely. Add the remaining ingredients and grind to blend.

MEATS

FROM CHICKEN-FRIED preparations with down-home gravy to savory stuffed dumplings, from succulent stir-fries to ribs, cutlets, and chops, we all have favorite fried meat dishes, which are fast becoming a secret indulgence in today's health-conscious world. Now we can once again enjoy these dishes without guilt thanks to hot-oven baking techniques that yield the taste and texture of deep-frying without the tons of oil and the telltale mess, nonstick surfaces that allow you to pan-fry and griddle up a storm without grease, and recipes that spare the oil without spoiling the stir-fry.

We've pared preparations of superfluous fat, but do bear in mind that meat itself is relatively high in fat. Choose only the leanest cuts, as directed in individual recipes. Never buy preground meat, which is often a considerable source of hidden fat. Start with lean cuts of well-trimmed beef sirloin or pork tenderloin, cut meat into small chunks, and put it into the bowl of a food processor. Pulse a few times to break it up, then process to a fine grind.

Chicken-Fried Steak

Breaded Veal Cutlets

Grandma's Chiles Rellenos

Beef and Spinach Goyza

Stir-Fried Pepper Steak

Meat and Potato Empanadas

Hoisin Beef Stir-Fried with Garlic

"Pan-Fried" Rabbit

Crusty Country Ribs

Bourbon Pork and Vegetable Stir-Fry

Fabulous Flautas

Chorizo: Light, but Right!

Ribs in Black Bean Sauce

Pork with Chinese Broccoli in Oyster Sauce

Unfried Pork Chops

Claudia's Country-Fried Cutlet

CHICKEN-FRIED STEAK

MAKES 4 SERVINGS

PER SERVING
Fat 6 g
Protein 31 g
Carbohydrates 25 g
Calories 290

The setting was Don's Eat and Barbecue, situated on the dusty main drag of one of the little Mississippi River towns west of Columbia in mid-Missouri. The time was the late 1970s—arguably before we knew better, although we probably did. The overflowing platters set in front of Kevin and his fellow traveler were weighted down with something called "chicken-fried steak," a breaded mass of meat surrounded by mounds of mashed potatoes and green beans, all doused with a prodigious helping of thick, white gravy. It was a bit intimidating and quite wonderful at the same time.

The enigmatically named chicken-fried steak is indeed a steak. Its only connection to chicken is in the typical style of preparation: breaded and fried. Also called country-fried steak, the artery-clogging dish is a favorite in cafes and diners spreading east from Texas into the South and north into the rural Midwest. Our hot-oven baked rendition can weigh down a plate with the best of them, despite its comparatively righteous nutritional breakdown. It even sports a pool of creamy gravy, in this case thickened with evaporated skim milk. We quake at the mere thought of what Don's chicken-fried steak must have contained in the way of fat and calories. (We recently saw a recipe for a supposedly reduced-fat version that had 40 grams of fat and 790 calories.) Our rendition has a mere 6 grams of fat and 290 calories.

Some supermarkets (even as far away from the Lone Star State as our neighborhood Chicago market) now sell a "thin" cut of the round sirloin tip steak. This is the cut used to make chicken-fried steak, which will save you the extra step of pounding the meat to the desired thickness of about ¼ inch.

1 pound boneless beef round sirloin tip steak

½ cup all-purpose flour

1 tablespoon garlic powder

1 teaspoon dried mustard

½ teaspoon salt

¼ teaspoon ground black pepper

⅓ cup potato starch

1 large egg white

1 tablespoon evaporated skim milk

2 teaspoons Worcestershire sauce

GRAVY

½ cup defatted chicken broth (canned or page 19)

½ cup evaporated skim milk

2 tablespoon all-purpose flour

½ teaspoon salt

⅛ teaspoon ground black pepper

Place a heavy-gauge nonstick baking sheet in the oven and preheat the oven to 475F (245C).

Trim and quarter the steak. Pound each quarter into a thin piece about ¼ inch thick, using a meat tenderizer, rubber mallet, or rolling pin.

On a large plate, mix together the flour, garlic powder, dried mustard, salt, and pepper. Sprinkle the potato starch onto a second plate. In a large, shallow bowl, lightly beat the egg white with the evaporated milk and Worcestershire sauce. Dip each piece of steak into the potato starch, shaking off excess starch. Dip it into the egg mixture, then coat evenly with the flour mixture.

Spray the preheated baking sheet with cooking spray. Put the steaks on the baking sheet and spray them lightly. Bake for 5 minutes. Turn the steaks over and bake until very well browned, about 5 minutes more.

Meanwhile, make the gravy. Combine the broth and evaporated milk in a microwave-safe container. Microwave on HIGH power until just steaming, about 1 minute. Put the flour into a heavy nonstick medium saucepan. Cook over medium heat, stirring constantly, until the flour is lightly toasted, about 3 minutes. Add the heated broth mixture, whisking to dissolve the flour. Cook for 7 to 8 minutes more, stirring frequently, until the gravy is thick and bubbly. Stir in the salt and pepper. Drizzle gravy over the steaks.

BREADED VEAL CUTLETS

Our rendition of the ever-popular veal parmigiana features a hint of sun-dried tomato in the breading in lieu of the typical layer of tomato sauce. Use veal leg cutlets for this recipe. The leanest cut of veal, the leg cutlet is pounded thin for veal scallopine. We happen to be partial to the slightly gamy taste of free-range veal.

Serve the cutlets with a simple risotto or with pasta or orzo tossed with basil.

MAKES 6 SERVINGS

PER SERVING
Fat 4.5 g
Protein 20 g
Carbohydrates 11 g
Calories 170

½ cup Italian-style breadcrumbs (prepared or page 23)

⅓ cup diced sun-dried tomatoes (see sidebar)

2 tablespoons all-purpose flour

1 large egg white

1 tablespoon water

6 (2½-ounce) veal leg cutlets

6 thin slices fontina cheese

Place a heavy-gauge nonstick baking sheet in the oven and preheat the oven to 450F (230C).

Combine the breadcrumbs and sun-dried tomatoes in the bowl of a food processor. Process until the tomatoes are finely chopped, 2 to 3 minutes. Transfer the mixture to a plate. Sprinkle the flour onto a second plate. Lightly beat the egg white and water in a large, shallow bowl.

Dust the cutlets in the flour, shaking off any excess. Dip them in the egg white mixture and turn them in the breadcrumb mixture to coat completely. Spray the preheated baking sheet with cooking spray, put the cutlets on the baking sheet, and bake for 5 minutes.

Coat the cutlets lightly with cooking spray, turn them over, and top each with a slice of cheese. Bake for about 2 minutes more, until the cheese has melted and begun to brown.

"SUN-DRYING" TOMATOES IN THE OVEN

Preheat the oven to 170F (75C). Line a baking sheet with foil. For 1 pound of sun-dried tomatoes, cut 5 pounds plum tomatoes in half lengthwise and place them, cut side up, on the lined baking sheet. Dry in the oven for about 6 hours, until the tomatoes are dry but still pliable; do not let them become brittle. Remove the tomatoes that are dry and put the rest back into the oven for up to 1 hour more. Let the tomatoes cool at room temperature before storing in an airtight container.

GRANDMA'S CHILES RELLENOS

MAKES 4 SERVINGS

PER SERVING
Fat 11 g
Protein 29 g
Carbohydrates 18 g
Calories 280

The inspiration for this recipe was a wonderful dish made by our friend Patty Oria's late grandmother, who learned to cook as a girl in Mexico. Grandma cooked her chiles rellenos in lard, spooning the lard over the chiles as they cooked, which made the coating puff up grandly. We approximate this phenomenon by folding egg whites that have been whipped to stiff peaks into our coating. Grandma always said to "use the Muenster," which she preferred to the somewhat blander varieties of Mexican cheese typically used in this dish.

We estimate that Grandma's original recipe probably weighed in at about 50 grams of fat and 590 calories per serving. Compare that with our 11 grams of fat and 280 calories!

HOW TO PREP THE CHILES

Preheat the broiler. Cover the rack with foil.

Place the chiles on the prepared rack and broil until charred, about 5 minutes per side. Remove the chiles to a plate, cover them loosely with a dish towel, and allow to cool enough to handle.

Rub off the chile skins. With the tip of a sharp knife make a slit down a flat side of each chile from just below the stem to about ½ inch above the tip. (Leave the stems intact.) Holding each chile under cold running water, carefully rinse out the seeds and cut the veins out with the tip of the knife. Do not pull the veins, which could rip the flesh of the chile.

6 ounces lean ground beef

6 ounces ground turkey

½ cup chopped yellow onion

2 cloves garlic, minced

¼ cup defatted beef broth (canned or page 21)

1 tablespoon cider vinegar

½ teaspoon dried oregano

¼ teaspoon salt

½ teaspoon ground black pepper

2 large eggs, separated

⅓ cup plus 1 tablespoon all-purpose flour

4 (6-ounce) poblano chiles, charred, seeded, and deveined (see sidebar)

4 (1-ounce) slices Muenster or mozzarella cheese

3 cups Tomato Broth (page 266)

Place a heavy-gauge nonstick baking sheet in the oven and preheat the oven to 450F (230C).

Meanwhile, make the filling. Preheat a medium nonstick skillet over medium-high heat. Add the beef, turkey, onion, and garlic. Sauté until the meat has browned, about 10 minutes. Stir in the beef broth, vinegar, oregano, salt, and pepper. Cook, stirring constantly, until the liquid has been absorbed, about 2 minutes. Remove from the heat and set aside.

Beat the egg whites to stiff peaks with an electric mixer at medium speed, about 2 minutes. Mix in the egg yolks and the 1 tablespoon of flour. Put the ⅓ cup flour on a plate.

Place about ⅓ cup of the filling in each chile. Top each with a slice of cheese and seal with a wooden toothpick. Dredge the stuffed chiles in the flour and shake off the excess. Spray the preheated baking sheet with cooking spray. Holding each chile by the stem, gently dip it into the egg mixture to coat and place on the baking sheet. Bake for 5 minutes.

Spray the chiles with cooking spray, carefully turn them over with a spatula, and bake about 5 minutes more, until well browned.

Remove the toothpicks and top each chile with about ¾ cup of the Tomato Broth.

BEEF AND SPINACH GOYZA

MAKES 4 SERVINGS

PER SERVING
Fat 4.5 g
Protein 13 g
Carbohydrates 21 g
Calories 180

These delectable little dumplings, also called pot stickers because they stick to the pot and become crusty on the bottom, are best served with Ginger Dipping Sauce (page 258). They're made with wonton skins—sometimes labeled wonton wrappers or dumpling wrappers—that can be found in the freezer case of most supermarkets. Check ingredient lists and choose a brand made without egg.

For a classic "poo poo platter" of the sort featured for years in Chinese restaurants, serve the goyza family style, along with Chili-Spiked Turkey Wontons (page 72), Ribs in Black Bean Sauce (page 52), and Rock Shrimp Spring Rolls (page 106). In addition to the Ginger Dipping Sauce, put out little bowls of Hoisin Dipping Sauce (page 257) and Soy Dipping Sauce (page 256).

8 ounces fresh baby spinach

6 ounces lean ground beef

1 large green onion, trimmed to white and light green parts and chopped (about 3 tablespoons)

1 tablespoon reduced-sodium soy sauce

2 teaspoons dry sherry

1 teaspoon hoisin sauce

16 round wonton skins

¼ cup plus 2 tablespoons water

Steam the spinach over boiling water until wilted, about 2 minutes. Squeeze excess water from the cooked spinach, chop, and put it in a large bowl.

Mix the beef and green onion with the spinach. Add the soy sauce, sherry, and hoisin sauce. Toss to mix, cover, and refrigerate for at least 5 minutes to firm.

In the center of each wonton skin, mound 1 scant tablespoon of the beef and spinach filling. Moisten the outer edge of the skin lightly with water. Fold the wonton in half over the filling and crimp the edges to seal securely.

Preheat a large nonstick skillet over high heat. Spray it twice with cooking spray and reduce the heat to medium. Place the goyza into the pan in a single layer and cook until the bottoms are well-browned and crusty, about 3 minutes. Add the water. Bring to a boil over high heat, cover, and steam for 3 minutes. Remove the cover and continue to cook until all water has evaporated, about 1 minute. Serve 4 goyza per person.

STIR-FRIED PEPPER STEAK

MAKES 4 SERVINGS

PER SERVING
Fat 7 g
Protein 27 g
Carbohydrates 17 g
Calories 250

This thoroughly modern and refreshing stir-fry bears little resemblance to either the pepper steak your mother cooked in her electric frying pan or the fat-laden dish of Chinese take-out. Our steak is cooked in a soy and sherry mixture; the accompanying vegetables, in water. Choose sirloin, which has more than a third less fat than tenderloin, and be sure to cut the peppers and onion into same size chunks so that they will cook uniformly. If your local supermarket doesn't stock the black bean sauce with garlic, look in an Asian grocery.

1 tablespoon reduced-sodium soy sauce

1 tablespoon dry sherry

2 tablespoons cornstarch

12 ounces boneless beef sirloin steak, trimmed and cut into 1-inch cubes

½ cup defatted chicken broth (canned or page 19)

3 tablespoons black bean sauce with garlic

½ tablespoon dark brown sugar

1 yellow onion, cut into ¾-inch chunks

1 red bell pepper, cored, seeded, and cut into ¾-inch chunks

1 green bell pepper, cored, seeded, and cut into ¾-inch chunks

¼ cup water

Combine the soy sauce, sherry, and 1 tablespoon of the cornstarch in a medium bowl. Toss the steak in the mixture and allow it to marinate at room temperature for 20 minutes.

For the sauce, combine the chicken broth, black bean sauce, brown sugar, and the remaining 1 tablespoon cornstarch in a small bowl. Mix and set aside.

Preheat a nonstick stir-fry pan, a large nonstick skillet, or a wok over high heat. Add the onion, bell peppers, and water. Cook, stirring constantly, until the onion has begun to color and all liquid has evaporated, about 5 minutes. Remove the vegetables and add the steak and its marinade to the pan. Cook, stirring constantly, until the meat is well browned, about 2 minutes. Add the reserved sauce mixture. Cook, stirring constantly, until the sauce is very thick and clear, about 1 minute. Return the vegetables to the pan and stir-fry for about 30 seconds more to coat.

MEAT AND POTATO EMPANADAS

MAKES 4 SERVINGS

PER SERVING
Fat 5 g
Protein 22 g
Carbohydrates 96 g
Calories 530

When we toured South America a few years ago, we enjoyed empanadas at every stop, from cosmopolitan Buenos Aires, where they are as popular as hot dogs are at home in Chicago, to otherworldly La Paz, where the locals call them *salteñas*. Think of these pastries as kissing cousins of the New York knish. Knishes are usually filled with either meat or potatoes; we fill our empanadas with both.

Although jerk seasoning, which accents the filling mixture, is usually associated with Jamaican cooking, it embodies the typical South American balance of sweet and savory quite well. Empanadas often are made with hot chiles, which can be a chore to seed and devein, and which not everyone digests easily, so we gave our rendition the requisite bit of heat by putting a little hot paprika in the crust.

Paired with a side salad, these generously proportioned, very aromatic pastries make a satisfying meal.

3 tablespoons buttermilk

1 large egg

2 egg whites

⅓ cup plus ½ tablespoon water

3 cups all-purpose flour

2 teaspoons hot paprika

4 ounces lean ground beef

1 red potato, peeled and diced (about 1 cup)

1 small yellow onion, chopped (about ¾ cup)

1 tablespoon jerk seasoning (prepared or page 27)

1 teaspoon ground cumin

⅓ cup golden raisins

½ cup breadcrumbs

¼ cup fresh cilantro leaves

Whisk the buttermilk, egg, 1 of the egg whites, and the ⅓ cup water together in a small bowl. In a large bowl, combine the flour and paprika. Stir the buttermilk mixture into the flour mixture to form a dough. Knead the dough into a smooth ball. Cover and refrigerate for 30 minutes.

Preheat a medium nonstick skillet. Add the meat, potato, onion, jerk seasoning, and cumin. Cover and cook over medium-low heat, stirring occasionally, until cooked through and very lightly browned, about 15 minutes. Remove from the heat, stir in the raisins, and set aside to cool.

Preheat the oven to 425F (220C). Combine the breadcrumbs and cilantro in the bowl of a food processor, process until finely ground, and remove to a plate. In a small bowl, combine the remaining egg white and the ½ tablespoon water.

Turn the dough out onto a lightly floured work surface and roll it out into a 16 × 12-inch rectangle. Cut it into 8 (6 × 4-inch) rectangles. In the center of each rectangle, mound ¼ cup of the meat and potato filling. Moisten the outer edges with the egg white and water wash. With lightly floured fingers, fold each rectangle in half over the filling and crimp to seal. Paint the empanadas on both sides with the egg wash and dredge them in the breadcrumb mixture.

Arrange the empanadas on a heavy-gauge nonstick baking sheet and bake for 10 minutes. Turn them over and bake for 10 to 12 minutes more, until golden brown all over. Serve each person 2 empanadas.

HOISIN BEEF STIR-FRIED WITH GARLIC

MAKES 4 SERVINGS

PER SERVING
Fat 5 g
Protein 17 g
Carbohydrates 22 g
Calories 200

This rich, garlicky stir-fry is cooked in beef broth, which enhances rather than overwhelms the flavor of the dish, instead of oil. The dish is flavored with hoisin sauce, which is stocked in the Asian section of many markets and by Asian groceries. It's best known as the moderately sweet, reddish-brown sauce spread on the pancakes that hold mu shu pork. Hoisin sauce is sold both in glass jars and in plastic squeeze bottles; the thicker variety that comes in a glass jar is preferable for this recipe. Serve the stir-fry with plain white rice or with Vegetable Fried Rice (page 186).

SAUCE

⅔ cup defatted beef broth (canned or page 21)

2 tablespoons hoisin sauce

1 tablespoon cornstarch

1 tablespoon reduced-sodium soy sauce

2 tablespoons chopped fresh basil

1 clove garlic, chopped

8 ounces beef flank steak, trimmed and thinly sliced across the grain

2 tablespoons dry sherry

1 teaspoon cornstarch

1½ tablespoons reduced-sodium soy sauce

¼ cup defatted beef broth (canned or page 21)

4 slices fresh ginger about the size of quarters, peeled

4 cloves garlic, peeled and smashed

8 ounces sugar snap peas

1 red bell pepper, cored, seeded, and cut into ¼-inch strips

1 thin leek, trimmed, cleaned, and thinly sliced

½ cup sliced bamboo shoots, drained

Combine all ingredients for the sauce in a small bowl, mix, and set aside.

In a medium bowl, combine the beef, sherry, cornstarch, and soy sauce. Mix well and set aside to marinate for 5 minutes.

Preheat a nonstick stir-fry pan, a large nonstick skillet, or a wok over high heat. Add the broth. As soon as it is steamy, add the ginger and garlic. Cook until about half the broth has evaporated, about 30 seconds. Add the sugar snap peas, bell pepper, and leek. Cook, stirring constantly, until the vegetables are lightly browned and all of the liquid has been absorbed, about 2 minutes. Add the bamboo shoots and cook, stirring, just to warm, about 10 seconds. Discard the ginger and garlic, and transfer the remaining contents of the pan to a bowl.

Reheat the pan. Add the beef and its marinade. Cook, stirring constantly, until the beef is cooked through, about 1 minute. Add the sauce and stir to liquefy any marinade that may have congealed. Cook, stirring, until the liquid thickens, bubbles, and turns clear, about 30 seconds more. Remove from the heat and stir in the vegetables.

"PAN-FRIED" RABBIT

MAKES 6 SERVINGS

PER SERVING
Fat 8 g
Protein 56 g
Carbohydrates 25 g
Calories 420

Although rabbit is the game animal most eaten in the United States, we can't understand why it isn't even more popular. Now farm-raised, it's almost all white meat, low in saturated fat and calories, and high in iron and other minerals. Most butcher shops and many supermarkets stock rabbit, both fresh and frozen.

In this recipe, rabbit is prepared in the style of the pan-fried dish long popular in rural America, especially in the South. Our hot-oven baking even produces crusty spots on the coating similar to those that would result from frying in a cast-iron skillet. We update the presentation somewhat with a light, stock-based sauce. For a more traditional feel, use the gravy from our Chicken-Fried Steak (page 30).

The flavor improves the longer the rabbit sits in the marinade. If you have the time, let it marinate in the refrigerator for up to 36 hours.

1½ cups buttermilk

¼ cup Dijon mustard

1 tablespoon onion powder

2½ teaspoons salt

1½ teaspoons ground black pepper

1 (3 to 3½-pound) rabbit, cut into 10 pieces (see sidebar, opposite)

1½ cups breadcrumbs

1½ cups all-purpose flour

1 tablespoon dried thyme or 3 tablespoons chopped fresh thyme

1 tablespoon dried mustard

Reserved lower forelegs and neck of rabbit (see sidebar, opposite)

1 cup defatted chicken broth (canned or page 19)

2 strips turkey bacon, cut into thin matchsticks

2 sprigs fresh thyme

⅛ teaspoon ground black pepper

Combine the buttermilk and Dijon mustard in a small bowl. Whisk to blend, then whisk in the onion powder, ½ teaspoon of the salt, and ½ teaspoon of the pepper. Pour the mixture into a heavy-duty plastic storage bag. Add the rabbit to the bag. Squeeze the air from the bag, seal tightly, and shake the bag to evenly coat the rabbit. Marinate in the refrigerator for 12 to 36 hours, gently shaking the bag occasionally.

Place a heavy-gauge nonstick baking sheet in the oven and preheat the oven to 475F (245C).

Mix the breadcrumbs, flour, dried thyme, dried mustard, the remaining 2 teaspoons salt, and 1 teaspoon pepper together thoroughly and sprinkle over a platter or tray. Turn each piece of rabbit in the flour mixture to coat well.

Spray the preheated baking sheet with cooking spray and place the rabbit on the sheet in a single layer. Bake for 15 minutes. Spray each piece of rabbit lightly with cooking spray, turn the pieces over, and spray again. Bake until the rabbit is well browned and the juices run clear when the meat is pierced with the tines of a fork, about 15 minutes more.

Meanwhile, for the sauce, preheat a small nonstick skillet over high heat. Spray the reserved rabbit pieces lightly with cooking spray and put them in the pan. Cook, turning the pieces occasionally, until they begin to brown, about 2 minutes. Cover, reduce the heat to low, and cook until well browned, about 25 minutes. Add the broth and scrape to dislodge the crusty bits from the bottom and sides of the pan. Increase the heat to high, bring to a boil, and boil for 5 minutes. Strain the broth through a sieve into a bowl and discard solids. (You should have about ¾ cup broth.)

Place the bacon in the skillet and sauté over medium heat until cooked through but not browned, 3 to 4 minutes. Return the strained broth to the skillet, along with the thyme sprigs and pepper. Heat the sauce until steaming. Discard the thyme before serving.

CUTTING UP A RABBIT

If you buy a fresh rabbit from a friendly butcher, you might be able to bring it home cut into serving pieces. We've also seen cut-up rabbit in the freezer case of gourmet markets. Otherwise, cut the rabbit into 10 pieces with a cleaver, large knife, or poultry shears as follows. First cut it crosswise into 3 segments: the hind legs, the saddle, and the forelegs. Cut the hind legs in half through the backbone and then separate each portion into leg and thigh. Cut the saddle in half crosswise, then cut each portion in half lengthwise, discarding the large flaps of excess skin. Separate the forelegs, removing and reserving the bony lower section of each foreleg, as well as the neck, for the sauce.

CRUSTY COUNTRY RIBS

MAKES 6 SERVINGS

PER SERVING
Fat 10 g
Protein 9 g
Carbohydrates 6 g
Calories 150

In this recipe, we've taken a traditional Mexican dish and given it a Chinese accent in the form of aromatic five-spice powder and a smidgen of sesame oil for added flavor. Serve three ribs per person as an appetizer, along with Apricot Mustard Dipping Sauce (page 255) and little bowls in which the bones can be discarded. We think your guests will approve. The baby back ribs are leaner than the typical sparerib and, in this presentation, quite a bit easier to eat than the usual barbecue preparation.

1 pound baby back pork loin ribs, cut in half horizontally by butcher

4 cups water

Dark green ends of 1 green onion

2 tablespoons all-purpose flour

1 large egg white

1 teaspoon sesame oil

½ cup breadcrumbs

1 tablespoon Chinese five-spice powder (prepared or page 25)

Lift the thin, opaque membrane off the back of the ribs with the tip of a knife and discard it. Cut the pieces into individual ribs. (You should have 16 to 18.)

Combine the water and green onion in a large saucepan. Bring to a boil over high heat, add the ribs, and cook for about 10 minutes. Remove the ribs and allow them to cool.

Place a heavy-gauge nonstick baking sheet in the oven and preheat the oven to 450F (230C).

Sprinkle the flour onto a plate. In a large, shallow bowl, lightly beat the egg white with the oil. Combine the breadcrumbs and five-spice powder in a plastic bag.

Dust the ribs with the flour and dip them in the egg white mixture. Shake 3 or 4 ribs at a time in the breadcrumb mixture to coat. Spray the preheated baking sheet with cooking spray, spray the ribs on all sides, and place them on the sheet. Bake for about 20 minutes, until well browned, turning the ribs every 5 minutes for even browning.

BOURBON PORK AND VEGETABLE STIR-FRY

MAKES 4 SERVINGS

PER SERVING
Fat 2 g
Protein 10 g
Carbohydrates 13 g
Calories 120

Bourbon gives a woody touch to this intriguing stir-fry and boosts the flavor of the pork. The alcohol burns off quickly in cooking, leaving only a hint of whiskey flavoring. In this recipe, we use thin-skinned plum tomatoes, which don't need to be peeled, as would their larger relatives, and are the perfect size for stir-frying when quartered. Cremini mushrooms, sometimes called brown buttons, are really baby portobellos. To clean, just wipe them or quickly rinse and dry. (Contrary to popular belief, it is not sacrilegious to wash mushrooms. Just don't let them sit in water for any length of time.)

SAUCE

¾ cup vegetable broth (canned or page 20)

2 teaspoons cornstarch

1 tablespoon hoisin sauce

1 tablespoon reduced-sodium soy sauce

4 ounces pork tenderloin, cut into about ¼-inch-thick strips

3 tablespoons bourbon

1 tablespoon cornstarch

½ cup vegetable broth (canned or page 20)

8 ounces asparagus, trimmed and cut on the diagonal into 3-inch pieces

4 ounces cremini mushrooms, sliced (about 2 cups)

4 plum tomatoes, quartered and seeded

¼ cup sliced fresh basil leaves

Combine all ingredients for the sauce in a small bowl and set aside.

In a large bowl, mix together the pork, bourbon, and cornstarch.

Preheat a nonstick stir-fry pan, a large nonstick skillet, or a wok over high heat. Add ¼ cup of the broth. Let heat for 1 minute, then add the asparagus and mushrooms. Cook, stirring constantly, until the mushrooms begin to brown and the asparagus turns bright green, about 2 minutes. Add the tomatoes and cook, stirring, for 30 seconds more. Remove the asparagus, mushrooms, and tomatoes to a bowl.

Add the remaining ¼ cup broth to the pan and bring to a boil. Add the sauce and cook, stirring constantly, until thickened, about 30 seconds. Add the pork and stir-fry until the meat is no longer pink, about 1 minute. Return the asparagus, mushrooms, and tomatoes to the pan. Cook, stirring, until the sauce is bubbly, about 1 minute more. Stir in the basil and serve.

FABULOUS FLAUTAS

MAKES 8 SERVINGS

PER SERVING (INCLUDING
CHORIZO)
Fat 3.5 g
Protein 16 g
Carbohydrates 17 g
Calories 170

Versatile flautas work just as well as party fare as they do in their original role as a typical after-work snack in Mexico. Serve two flautas per person as an appetizer. Add a side of rice and Refried Beans (page 182) for an entree, or heap the flautas on a platter as hors d'oeuvres.

Not only do we bake rather than deep-fry our healthier rendition, but we also make our own light chorizo from a turkey and pork mixture for the filling, instead of the fat-laden stuff sold in the supermarket. The toothpicks help the flautas hold their classic cigar shape as the tortillas crisp; don't forget to remove them before serving. *Queso fresco* is similar to farmer cheese.

16 white corn tortillas

2 cups cooked chorizo (see opposite)

⅓ cup grated *queso fresco*

2 tablespoons plus 2 teaspoons chopped fresh cilantro

Preheat the oven to 450F (230C). Spray a heavy-gauge nonstick baking sheet with cooking spray.

Spray both sides of a tortilla with cooking spray. Mound 2 tablespoons of the chorizo, 1 teaspoon of the grated cheese, and ½ teaspoon of the cilantro on one side of the tortilla. Roll the tortilla tightly around the filling in a cigar-shaped cylinder, and secure closed with 2 or 3 wooden toothpicks. Repeat the process to fill and assemble 15 more flautas.

Place the flautas on the prepared baking sheet and spray them with cooking spray. Bake for 7 minutes, turn the flautas over, and bake for about 3 minutes more, until very crisp and well browned.

CHORIZO: LIGHT, BUT RIGHT!

(Use this light and healthy homemade sausage in Fabulous Flautas (opposite), Breakfast Burritos (page 202), or in tacos, or serve with scrambled eggs.

½ pound ground turkey

½ pound ground pork

2 tablespoons red wine vinegar

¼ teaspoon green hot sauce

½ tablespoon hot paprika

½ tablespoon chili powder

1 teaspoon salt

½ teaspoon ground cumin

¼ teaspoon ground coriander

¼ teaspoon ground black pepper

MAKES 2 CUPS;
8 SERVINGS

PER SERVING
(CHORIZO ONLY)
Fat 1.5 g
Protein 13 g
Carbohydrates 1 g
Calories 70

Combine all ingredients in a large bowl and mix well.

Preheat a medium nonstick skillet over medium-high heat. Add the turkey mixture and cook, stirring with a fork to distribute the meat evenly over the bottom of the pan. Stirring constantly, cook until the meat is lightly browned and crumbly, about 5 minutes.

RIBS IN BLACK BEAN SAUCE

MAKES 8 SERVINGS

PER SERVING
Fat 10 g
Protein 9 g
Carbohydrates 3 g
Calories 140

Use baby back loin ribs, which are leaner and tenderer than spareribs, for this dim sum appetizer favorite. Your butcher can cut the slab in half horizontally for you, which will yield diminutive ribs of just the right proportions. We dry-fry the ribs, which have enough fat to brown beautifully without the addition of oil. Serve over Vegetable Fried Rice (page 186) alongside Gingered Stir-Fried Vegetables (page 168) as a main course.

1½ pounds baby back pork loin ribs, cut in half horizontally by butcher

4 cups water

Dark green ends of 1 green onion

3 (2 x 1-inch) pieces fresh ginger, peeled

1 large clove garlic, smashed

SAUCE

½ cup defatted chicken broth (canned or page 19)

¼ cup black bean sauce with garlic

2 green onions (light green and white parts), cut on the diagonal into ½-inch pieces

1 tablespoon dark brown sugar

1 tablespoon grated fresh ginger

Lift the thin, opaque membrane off the back of the ribs with the tip of a knife and discard it. Cut the pieces into individual ribs. (You should have 22 to 24.)

Combine the water, green onion, ginger, and garlic in a large saucepan. Bring to a boil over high heat, add the ribs, reduce heat, and simmer until cooked through, about 25 minutes. Remove the ribs and set them aside.

Combine all ingredients for the sauce in a small bowl and mix.

Preheat a nonstick stir-fry pan, a large nonstick skillet, or a wok over high heat. Add the ribs and cook, stirring occasionally, until well browned, 3 to 5 minutes. Add the sauce and cook, stirring constantly, until the sauce has been absorbed and the ribs are nicely glazed, about 3 minutes more.

PORK WITH CHINESE BROCCOLI IN OYSTER SAUCE

MAKES 6 SERVINGS

PER SERVING
Fat 2.5 g
Protein 15 g
Carbohydrates 18 g
Calories 150

We keep the fat in this flavorful dish to a minimum by cooking the meat in soy sauce and the vegetables in water. Look for the oyster sauce in the Asian section of your supermarket. Although most markets now stock fresh shiitake mushrooms, you could also use dried; start with 1 ounce dried mushrooms and reconstitute by soaking them in hot water for about 30 minutes. If you can't find Chinese broccoli, substitute the equally pungent Italian broccoli rabe, or rapini, rather than the blander regular variety.

SAUCE

¼ cup oyster sauce

2 tablespoons dry sherry

½ teaspoon sugar

12 ounces pork tenderloin, cut into about ¼-inch-thick strips

1 tablespoon reduced-sodium soy sauce

1 large red bell pepper, cored, seeded, and cut into strips

8 ounces Chinese broccoli, cut into 2-inch chunks

¼ cup water

1 teaspoon grated fresh ginger

1 large clove garlic, minced

4 ounces shiitake mushrooms, trimmed, cleaned, and halved

Combine all ingredients for the sauce in a small bowl. Mix and set aside.

Preheat a nonstick stir-fry pan, a large nonstick skillet, or a wok over medium heat. Add the pork and soy sauce, and cook, stirring constantly, until the pork is no longer pink and the soy sauce has been absorbed, about 1 minute. Remove the pork and add the bell pepper, Chinese broccoli, and water to the pan. Increase the heat to medium-high, and stir-fry until the broccoli turns bright green, about 2 minutes. Add the ginger and garlic, and cook, stirring, for about 1 minute. Stir in the mushrooms and cook for about 20 seconds more, until all liquid has been absorbed.

Return the pork to the pan, along with the sauce. Cook, stirring, to heat through and coat the pork, about 20 seconds.

UNFRIED PORK CHOPS

MAKES 4 SERVINGS

PER SERVING
Fat 8 g
Protein 26 g
Carbohydrates 28 g
Calories 290

We had the pleasure of working with Rosie Daley a few years ago on her best-selling cookbook, *In the Kitchen with Rosie.* Rosie coined the phrase "unfried" to describe her healthy, baked renditions of such foods as French fries and fried chicken, which turned out to be some of the most popular recipes in her book.

We've borrowed Rosie's clever terminology to describe our version of the archetypal Midwestern pork chop dinner. Instead of frying the chops in fat, as is usually done, we "unfry" them in the oven, paring the fat while retaining the texture and taste of fried. For "smothered" Southern pork chops, top the chops with gravy from Claudia's Country-Fried Cutlet (page 58). We like to serve Unfried Pork Chops with a little Apple Chutney (page 265) on the side. Vinegar and Salt French Fries (page 156), Polenta-Encrusted Fried Green Tomatoes (page 170), or Creole Okra (page 177) would make a good accompaniment.

Sometimes we substitute boneless top loin chops for center-cut pork chops and serve them in kaiser rolls, just as they do at the lively flea market that draws crowds from throughout the Midwest to the little town of Sandwich, Illinois. Folks make their first trip to Sandwich to shop the market, and return for the fried pork chop sandwiches.

1½ cups breadcrumbs

½ teaspoon salt

¼ teaspoon ground black pepper

¼ cup all-purpose flour

1 teaspoon garlic powder

2 large egg whites

1 tablespoon water

4 (6-ounce) center-cut pork chops

Place a heavy-gauge nonstick baking sheet in the oven and preheat the oven to 500F (260C).

Mix the breadcrumbs, salt, and pepper together on a plate. On a second plate, combine the flour and garlic powder. Beat the egg whites and water lightly in a large, shallow bowl.

Dredge the pork chops in the flour, shaking off any excess. Dip them in the egg white mixture and then turn them in the breadcrumb mixture to coat completely. Spray the preheated baking sheet lightly with cooking spray. Put the pork chops on the baking sheet and place on the bottom oven rack. Bake for 10 minutes.

Spray the pork chops lightly with cooking spray, turn them over, and bake 8 to 10 minutes more, until well browned and cooked through at the bone.

CLAUDIA'S COUNTRY-FRIED CUTLET

MAKES 4 SERVINGS

PER SERVING
Fat 4.5 g
Protein 24 g
Carbohydrates 28 g
Calories 260

Our friend Claudia Clark Potter lives on Cedar Creek Lake, down the road a piece from Gun Barrel City, Texas, and up the street from the Feed Box restaurant, where the food is always fried, the biscuits are awash with gravy, and the pies are made fresh every day.

We created this healthful hybrid—which is not on the menu at the Feed Box—for Claudia, who loves pork. Think of it as country-fried steak without the steak and without the "fried." Inspired by Texas's beloved country-fried, or chicken-fried, steak, which is prepared in the manner of fried chicken, we have substituted a lean boneless pork chop for the usual beefsteak, and crisped the spicy breading in a hot oven instead of in a skillet of hot oil.

The gravies that always accompany country-fried dishes usually start with cooking flour in high-fat pan drippings. We make our equally rich renditions by stirring thick, creamy evaporated skim milk mixtures into flour that has been toasted by dry-frying.

2 (5- to 6-ounce) boneless pork loin chops

1 large egg white

¼ cup plus 1 tablespoon water

¼ cup all-purpose flour

½ teaspoon poultry seasoning (prepared or page 28)

½ cup all-purpose buttermilk baking mix

½ teaspoon salt

½ teaspoon ground black pepper

1 cup evaporated skim milk

¼ cup water

Place a heavy-gauge nonstick baking sheet in the oven and preheat the oven to 450F (230C).

Cut the pork chops in half crosswise. Place the pieces on a cutting board, cover with wax paper, and pound to ¼-inch thickness.

In a large, shallow bowl, lightly beat the egg white and the 1 tablespoon water. Mix the flour and poultry seasoning together on a plate. Combine the baking mix, salt, and pepper on another plate. Dip each piece of pork into the flour mixture, shaking off excess flour and reserving the mixture. Dip them in the egg mixture, then turn to coat all over in the seasoned baking mix.

Spray the preheated baking sheet with cooking spray. Place the pieces of pork on the baking sheet, spray them lightly with cooking spray, and bake for 5 minutes. Spray again, turn the pork, and bake for about 5 minutes more, until well browned.

For the gravy, combine the evaporated milk and the ¼ cup water in a microwave-safe container, cover, and microwave for about 1 minute on HIGH power, until it begins to steam. Put 2 tablespoons of the reserved flour and poultry seasoning mixture in a heavy, non-stick medium saucepan. Cook over medium heat, stirring constantly, until it begins to color, about 2 minutes. Whisk in the evaporated milk mixture. Cook, stirring often, until the gravy thickens and comes to a boil, 7 to 8 minutes more. Serve the gravy over the pork or on the side.

Claudia's Mashed Potatoes

MAKES 4 SERVINGS

PER SERVING
Fat 1 g
Protein 3 g
Carbohydrates 22 g
Calories 100

The natural accompaniment to country-fried food, and the only thing Claudia likes better than her pork cutlets, is mashed potatoes.

1 parsnip, peeled and cut into chunks

2 tablespoons grated fresh horseradish

8 ounces Yukon Gold potatoes (about 2 potatoes), cut into chunks

¼ teaspoon salt

⅛ teaspoon ground white pepper

¼ cup buttermilk

2 tablespoons reduced-fat sour cream

Bring a large saucepan of water to a boil over high heat. Add the parsnip and horseradish. Cook for 5 minutes. Add the potato and cook until vegetables are tender, about 15 minutes more. Drain and transfer the mixture to a large bowl. Add the salt, pepper, buttermilk, and sour cream. Mash and serve.

POULTRY

WE'VE HEARD SO much in recent years about how healthy poultry is that we tend to think of every bite of chicken or turkey as benign, if not actually health-promoting. And we're basically right insofar as the skinless, boneless chicken breast on its way to the broiler or the turkey tenderloin standing in for corned beef in a sandwich are concerned. But place that innocent piece of poultry in a vat of hot oil, or even an innocuous-seeming wok with the typical dose of oil used to stir-fry, and there's usually trouble right here in fat gram city!

For our re-creations of the classics, from buttermilk "fried" chicken to Buffalo-style nibbles, poultry curries to crispy little game birds, we have in most cases removed the skin, the biggest impediment to healthful eating. You could leave it on and still pare fat by virtue of skirting the deep-fryer, but it really isn't needed, since the crunch in these dishes comes from the crumb. When preground turkey is called for, follow the path of least fat. Select turkey breast tenderloin and have your butcher grind it, or grind it at home, following the directions on page 29.

MRS. JACKSON'S OLD-FASHIONED BUTTERMILK FRIED CHICKEN

MAKES 6 SERVINGS

PER SERVING
Fat 6 g
Protein 38 g
Carbohydrates 31 g
Calories 350

This is down-home Southern "fried" chicken like that made by Mrs. Jackson, the mother of a colleague from Barry's days at Motown. In addition to raising three Grammy- or Emmy-winning daughters, Mrs. Jackson was an award-winning cook in Barry's mind. She taught him the old trick of using buttermilk, which softens and tenderizes the meat.

Buttermilk is even more useful in these health-conscious days of skinless chicken. It coats the chicken much like a new skin, sealing in natural juices. We recently served friends chicken prepared according to this recipe, mixing in some pieces still bearing skin beneath the coating with the skinless pieces, and they were unable to tell the difference. Our best guess is that Mrs. Jackson's fried chicken most likely had about 34 grams of fat and 500 calories per serving, compared with our 6 grams of fat and 350 calories.

Plan ahead if possible, since this chicken is better after marinating a second day in the refrigerator. To carry out the Southern theme, top the chicken with some country gravy. We suggest the gravy from our Chicken-Fried Chicken (page 66).

1 (3- to 3½-pound) fryer chicken, cut into 8 pieces

2½ cups buttermilk

2 cloves garlic, smashed

⅓ cup Dijon mustard

1¾ teaspoons salt

1½ cups breadcrumbs

1½ cups all-purpose flour

¼ teaspoon cayenne pepper

½ tablespoon paprika

Remove the skin from all pieces of the chicken except the wings, and put the chicken into a heavy-duty plastic storage bag. Add the buttermilk, garlic, mustard, and ¾ teaspoon of the salt. Squeeze the air from the bag, seal tightly, and shake the bag to evenly coat the chicken. Marinate in the refrigerator for 24 to 48 hours, gently shaking the bag periodically.

Preheat the oven to 475F (245C). Spray a heavy-gauge nonstick baking sheet with cooking spray.

Mix the breadcrumbs, flour, cayenne, paprika, and the remaining 1 teaspoon salt together on a plate. Drain the chicken. Turn each piece of chicken in the breadcrumb mixture to coat all over and place, bone side up, on the prepared baking sheet. Let sit for 5 minutes, then spray the chicken to coat lightly with cooking spray.

Place the baking sheet on the bottom rack of the oven and bake for 20 minutes. Turn the pieces of chicken over with a spatula, taking care not to dislodge any coating, and reposition the sheet in the middle of the oven. Bake until the chicken is well browned, about 20 minutes more.

Lemon Mustard Chicken for Olivia

MAKES 4 SERVINGS

PER SERVING
Fat 4.5 g
Protein 19 g
Carbohydrates 7 g
Calories 150

Admittedly, we've always looked askance at recipes whose ingredient lists include cornflakes. But when a journalist acquaintance in Kansas City complained, "All of those ersatz fried recipes that start with cornflakes taste like cornflakes, not like fried," the challenge got too great. We simply had to create a cornflake formula that worked—and we're convinced we did in this recipe, in which the pungent mustard, lemon, and pepper mix of the marinade overshadows the cornflakes, which provide more texture than taste. What do you think, Olivia?

This chicken is very good at room temperature, making it a likely candidate for buffets and picnics. It goes well with Southern Cabbage Slaw (page 137) and Cajun Steak House Potatoes (page 160), or almost any of our chips. Chicken breasts could easily be substituted for the thighs.

1 large egg

2 tablespoons Dijon mustard

1 tablespoon fresh lemon juice

1 teaspoon ground black pepper

4 skinless, boneless chicken thighs (about 12 ounces total), halved crosswise

1½ cups cornflakes

½ tablespoon finely grated lemon zest

Whisk the egg and mustard together in a medium bowl. Mix in the lemon juice and pepper. Add the chicken, cover, and marinate in the refrigerator for at least 1 hour.

Preheat the oven to 450F (230C).

Meanwhile, put the cornflakes between 2 sheets of wax paper and crush them with a rolling pin. Transfer the crumbs to a plate and mix in the lemon zest. Place a chicken thigh on top of the crumbs. With dry fingertips, push the thigh into the crumbs, turning to coat all over. Repeat the process for the remaining thighs.

Spray a heavy-gauge nonstick baking sheet with cooking spray. Place the thighs on the baking sheet and spray to coat them lightly. Bake for 8 minutes. Gently turn the thighs over and bake until golden brown, about 8 minutes more. Serve 2 pieces per person.

CHICKEN-FRIED CHICKEN

MAKES 4 SERVINGS

PER SERVING
Fat 3.5 g
Protein 33 g
Carbohydrates 37 g
Calories 320

We love the novelty of this dish—it's fried chicken made like fried steak that's made like fried chicken, which isn't exactly like plain old-fashioned fried chicken. And then you have to consider the fact that it's baked, not fried, in the first place. The bottom line is that it's good; you have our word for that. Stop trying to figure it out and just try it.

The gravy's also a bit unusual. A healthy rendition of an old-fashioned white gravy made with evaporated skim milk and broth, it has just enough cayenne to set it apart. If you have all the ingredients for the gravy ready, you can start it when the chicken goes into the oven, and it will be ready and steaming by the time the chicken comes out.

Some supermarkets now carry thin chicken cutlets, or chicken scallopine, just the right thickness for this recipe. You could also substitute turkey tenderloin slices.

4 (4-ounce) skinless, boneless chicken breast halves

1 large egg white

2 tablespoons skim milk

⅓ cup all-purpose flour

¾ teaspoon dried thyme

1 cup all-purpose buttermilk baking mix

½ tablespoon paprika

1 teaspoon salt

¼ teaspoon cayenne pepper

GRAVY

1 cup defatted chicken broth (canned or page 19)

½ cup skim milk

3 tablespoons all-purpose flour

½ teaspoon salt

⅛ teaspoon cayenne pepper

Place a heavy-gauge nonstick baking sheet in the oven and preheat the oven to 500F (260C).

Place the chicken breasts between sheets of wax paper and pound until very thin with a meat tenderizer or rubber mallet.

In a large, shallow bowl, beat the egg white lightly with the skim milk. Combine the flour and thyme on a plate. On another plate, mix together the baking mix, paprika, salt, and cayenne. Dip the chicken breasts into the flour, shaking off excess. Dip them into the egg and milk mixture. Turn the breasts in the baking mix mixture to coat evenly.

Spray the preheated baking sheet with cooking spray. Lay the breasts on the baking sheet and bake for 5 minutes. Spray the chicken lightly, turn, and bake for about 5 minutes more, until just beginning to brown.

For the gravy, combine the broth and milk in a microwave-safe container and microwave on HIGH power for about 1½ minutes, until steaming. Preheat a heavy nonstick medium saucepan over medium heat. Add the flour and cook, stirring constantly, just until it begins to toast, about 3 minutes. Whisk in the broth and milk mixture, salt, and cayenne. Stirring frequently, cook for 8 to 10 minutes more, until the gravy is thick and bubbly. Drizzle gravy over the chicken breasts.

MOROCCAN CHICKEN

MAKES 4 SERVINGS

PER SERVING
Fat 4.5 g
Protein 21 g
Carbohydrates 26 g
Calories 230

The carrot juice marinade and heavy cumin accent of this dish are so evocative of flavorful and aromatic Moroccan cuisine that we simply have to serve it with couscous (see opposite). You could also serve it with Eggplant Panini (page 174) or Griddled Risotto Cakes (page 184).

Use organic carrot juice, which you can buy fresh in natural or health food stores, or frozen in natural food stores and some supermarkets, if you don't have your own juicer. Although it's a bit indulgent to use chicken thighs in lieu of leaner breast meat, the stronger, richer flavor of the dark meat is perfectly suited to the sweetness of the carrot and the robustness of the seasoning.

4 skinless, boneless chicken thighs (about 12 ounces total)

1 cup carrot juice

1 tablespoon ground cumin

½ tablespoon onion powder

½ cup all-purpose flour

½ cup breadcrumbs

1 tablespoon finely chopped fresh cilantro

1 teaspoon paprika

¾ teaspoon ground coriander

Cut each chicken thigh in half crosswise and place in a heavy-duty storage bag. In a small bowl, mix together the carrot juice, cumin, and onion powder. Add the mixture to the chicken, squeeze excess air from the bag, seal, and shake to coat. Marinate in the refrigerator for at least 2 hours.

Place a heavy-gauge nonstick baking sheet in the oven and preheat the oven to 450F (230C).

Sprinkle the flour on a plate. On a second plate, mix together the breadcrumbs, cilantro, paprika, and coriander. Dip each piece of chicken into the flour, shaking off the excess, and then roll the chicken in the breadcrumb mixture to coat all over.

Spray the preheated baking sheet lightly with cooking spray. Place the chicken on the baking sheet and spray it lightly with cooking spray. Bake for 8 minutes. Turn the chicken over and bake for about 8 minutes more, until golden brown.

Moroccan Couscous

Serve with Moroccan Chicken (opposite).

1½ cups defatted chicken broth (canned or page 19)

1 cup quick-cooking couscous

¼ cup diced carrot

¼ cup diced zucchini

2 tablespoons chopped fresh parsley

½ teaspoon curry powder

Put the broth into a small saucepan and bring to a boil over high heat. Stir in the couscous, carrot, zucchini, parsley, and curry powder. Cover, remove from the heat, and let stand for 5 minutes. Stir and serve.

MAKES 4 SERVINGS

PER SERVING
Fat 0 g
Protein 3 g
Carbohydrates 11 g
Calories 60

SHERI'S MOLE CHICKEN

MAKES 4 SERVINGS

PER SERVING
Fat 3 g
Protein 32 g
Carbohydrates 18 g
Calories 230

We came up with this dish to serve Barry's niece, Sheri, who's been pining for Southwestern food ever since she moved from Albuquerque to Portland. It features a rich yet mild mole.

Ancho chiles are readily available. Should you be lucky enough to find chipotles, which lend a wonderfully spicy smokiness to the recipe, by all means do not hesitate to use them in place of the anchos. You'll need about 10 of the dark reddish-brown chipotles, which are smaller than anchos. Whichever variety you use, select dried chiles that are flexible, not old and brittle.

Muenster or mozzarella cheese can easily be used in place of the Mexican cheese.

2 large dried ancho chiles (about 1 ounce total)

1½ cups boiling water

1 large clove garlic, peeled

½ teaspoon ground coriander

¼ teaspoon ground cinnamon

2 tablespoons tomato paste

¼ teaspoon salt

⅛ teaspoon cayenne pepper

2 tablespoons all-purpose flour

½ cup breadcrumbs

1 teaspoon dried thyme

½ teaspoon onion powder

2 large egg whites

4 (4-ounce) boneless, skinless chicken breast halves

4 slices *queso fresco*

Soak the chiles in the boiling water until softened, about 30 minutes.

Place a heavy-gauge nonstick baking sheet in the oven and pre-heat the oven to 500F (260C).

Meanwhile, remove the chiles from their soaking liquid and reserve the liquid. Core, seed, and devein the chiles. To make the mole, put the chiles into the bowl of a food processor, along with the garlic, coriander, and cinnamon. Add 1 cup of the soaking liquid and process until smooth. Transfer the contents of the bowl to a medium saucepan. Stir in the tomato paste, salt, and cayenne. Cook over medium-low heat until the sauce is thick, about 20 minutes. Cover and keep warm over low heat until ready to use.

Put the flour on a plate. On a second plate, combine the bread-crumbs, thyme, and onion powder. Beat the egg whites lightly in a large, shallow bowl. Dredge the chicken pieces in the flour, shaking off excess. Dip them in the egg whites and then in the breadcrumbs mixture, turning to coat evenly.

Spray the preheated baking sheet with cooking spray, place the chicken pieces on the baking sheet, and spray them lightly with cooking spray. Bake for 15 minutes.

Spread 3 tablespoons of the mole on each chicken piece and top with a slice of cheese. Bake 3 to 4 minutes, until the cheese has melted and lightly browned.

CHILI-SPIKED TURKEY WONTONS

MAKES 15 WONTONS

PER WONTON
Fat 0 g
Protein 3 g
Carbohydrates 5 g
Calories 35

You won't miss the oil one bit in these crisp, crunchy, baked wontons. These appetizers, which are very spicy, pair well with Ribs in Black Bean Sauce (page 52). We like to cool them down with some sauce on the side—Soy Dipping Sauce (page 256), Ginger Dipping Sauce (page 258), and Apricot Mustard Dipping Sauce (page 255) all work nicely—and a good dry sake on the rocks.

Look in the freezer section of your market for the wonton skins, which are now widely available. (We even prevailed upon the corner Chinese restaurant to sell us a few when we ran out late at night.) Look for a brand made without egg. The robust chili paste with garlic can be found in the Asian section of some supermarkets and in Asian groceries.

4 ounces ground turkey

1½ tablespoons diced green onion (light green and white parts)

2 tablespoons minced water chestnuts

1 tablespoon chopped fresh cilantro

½ teaspoon grated fresh ginger

⅛ teaspoon ground black pepper

1 teaspoon chili paste with garlic

1 teaspoon reduced-sodium soy sauce

½ teaspoon sesame oil

15 square wonton skins

Place a heavy-gauge nonstick baking sheet in the oven and preheat the oven to 475F (245C).

Combine the turkey, green onion, water chestnuts, cilantro, ginger, pepper, chili paste, soy sauce, and sesame oil in a medium bowl and mix thoroughly. Place 2 teaspoons of the mixture in the center of each wonton skin. Moisten 2 adjoining borders of the wonton skin with water and fold the skin over the filling to form a triangle. Press along the edges to seal.

Spray the preheated baking sheet with cooking spray. Place the wontons on the baking sheet and spray each lightly with cooking spray. Bake for 3 minutes. Turn the wontons over and bake about 2 minutes more, until browned and crispy.

SMOKED TURKEY HUSH PUPPIES

MAKES 4 SERVINGS

PER SERVING
Fat 1 g
Protein 16 g
Carbohydrates 35 g
Calories 210

Dolloped with Green Tomato Tartar (page 248) and served with a Caesar salad, mixed green salad, or bowl of soup, these generously proportioned hush puppies make a satisfying lunch or supper. They're best piping hot, right out of the oven.

Use smoked turkey sold on the bone, which is far superior to the typical pressed variety, if you can find it. Our supermarket stocks it next to hams. We use sweet paprika in this recipe, but you could easily substitute hot paprika if you are a lover of things hot and spicy. In any event, look for superior imported Hungarian paprika. Most supermarkets carry it. If yours doesn't stock hot paprika, look in a Middle Eastern market or a gourmet shop.

1¼ cups all-purpose flour

1 teaspoon baking powder

½ tablespoon poultry seasoning (prepared or page 28)

¾ teaspoon paprika

½ teaspoon salt

2 large egg whites

½ cup skim milk

8 ounces smoked turkey breast meat, diced (about 1 generous cup)

⅓ cup diced celery

2 tablespoons minced green onion (white and light green parts)

Place a heavy-gauge nonstick baking sheet in the oven and preheat the oven to 500F (260C).

Combine the flour, baking powder, poultry seasoning, paprika, and salt in a small bowl.

Combine the egg whites and milk in a large bowl. Whisk until frothy. Add the turkey, celery, and green onion, and stir to combine. Slowly stir in the flour mixture.

Spray the preheated baking sheet lightly with cooking spray.

Drop 8 hush puppies onto the sheet, using about ¼ cup of the mixture for each. Spray with cooking spray. Bake for 5 minutes.

Turn the hush puppies over, spray them on the other side, and bake for 4 to 5 minutes more, until browned. Serve 2 hush puppies per person.

THAI TURKEY CURRY

MAKES 4 SERVINGS

PER SERVING
Fat 1 g
Protein 22 g
Carbohydrates 10 g
Calories 140

TECHNIQUES OF WOKING

- **Always preheat your stir-fry pan, skillet, or wok before starting to add ingredients. When drops of water sizzle upon hitting the surface of the pan, it's ready.**

- **The first liquid typically put into the pan is peanut oil. For our healthy stir-fries, we start with water or stock, sometimes flavored with pieces of ginger and garlic.**

- **Follow directions for the successive addition of ingredients carefully; different ingredients take different times to cook. Unless otherwise directed, cut all ingredients for the stir-fry to about**

Thai red curry paste is just one of an ever-widening range of robust, low-fat Asian sauces and flavorings that have become readily available in recent years. The paste is bottled by the manufacturer that produces a broad line of Thai condiments that are now stocked by many supermarkets. It lends this dish quite a kick, along with a rich, red-orange color. Fish sauce, which can be found in some supermarkets and in Asian groceries, adds complexity and quietly boosts the flavor of other ingredients, much as the addition of a small quantity of anchovy does in Italian recipes.

Stir-fried the old-fashioned way in oil, this dish would have had 22 grams of fat, rather than just 1 gram!

The trick to successful stir-frying is to cut all ingredients into pieces of about the same size, to promote even cooking. Longer-cooking ingredients, such as the green beans in this recipe, are precooked a bit before the stir-fry is started.

SAUCE

2 teaspoons cornstarch

1 tablespoon fish sauce

1 tablespoon red curry paste

1 cup defatted chicken broth (canned or page 19)

10 ounces turkey breast tenderloin, cut into thin strips

1 tablespoon cornstarch

2 tablespoons fish sauce

1 tablespoon fresh lemon juice

4 ounces green beans

¼ cup plus 2 tablespoons defatted chicken broth (canned or page 19)

2 pieces fresh ginger about the size of quarters, peeled

1 clove garlic, peeled

1 small yellow onion, peeled and cut into thin wedges

1 red bell pepper, cored, seeded, and cut into long strips

½ cup sliced bamboo shoots, drained

¼ cup chopped fresh cilantro

Combine all ingredients for the sauce in a small bowl and mix thoroughly. In a medium bowl, combine the turkey, cornstarch, fish sauce, and lemon juice. Set aside.

Put the green beans into a microwave-safe container, cover loosely with plastic wrap, and microwave on HIGH power until steaming, about 1 minute. Leave covered until ready to use.

Preheat a nonstick stir-fry pan, a large nonstick skillet, or a wok over high heat. Combine the ¼ cup broth, the ginger, and garlic in the hot pan. Stir-fry for 30 seconds. Add the onion, bell pepper, and bamboo shoots. Cook until the onion is translucent, stirring constantly, about 2 minutes. Add the green beans. Cook, stirring, until the bamboo shoots have just begun to brown, about 1 minute more. Transfer the contents of the pan to a bowl, discarding the ginger and garlic.

Combine the remaining 2 tablespoons broth and the turkey mixture in the pan. Cook, stirring constantly, until the turkey is no longer pink, about 2 minutes. Add the sauce and cook, stirring, for about 1 minute more, until thick and bubbly. Return the vegetables to the pan and toss to coat with sauce. Garnish with the cilantro.

the same size.

- Stir-fry with two wooden spatulas or paddles (flat utensils with tapered scraping edges)—one in each hand—moving food up from the bottom of the pan, tossing, and turning it over to facilitate even cooking.

- Add the sauce to the stir-fry by pouring it slowly all around the pan and then tossing quickly to mix. (If you just dump the sauce into the center of the pan, the high heat could cause it to clump.)

- Remove the wok from the heat as soon as the stir-fry is cooked.

SAVORY TURKEY PASTRIES

MAKES 12 PASTRIES

PER PASTRY
Fat 1 g
Protein 5 g
Carbohydrates 12 g
Calories 80

Brazilians would make these little appetizers, called *empanaditas* in South America, with palm oil, which is second only to coconut oil in saturated fat. We use creamy low-fat buttermilk instead. The dough is soft enough that breadcrumbs will adhere, even without a wash or glaze, when the pastries are assembled on a breadcrumb-strewn surface. Serve with Cumin Mayonnaise (page 253).

1 cup plus 2 tablespoons all-purpose flour

½ teaspoon salt

⅓ cup buttermilk

1 large egg, lightly beaten

4 ounces ground turkey

⅓ cup chopped yellow onion

½ tablespoon jerk seasoning (prepared or page 27)

⅓ cup breadcrumbs

Place a heavy-gauge nonstick baking sheet in the oven and preheat the oven to 425F (220C).

Combine the flour and salt in a medium bowl. Mix in the buttermilk and egg to form a dough. Knead into a smooth ball, wrap in plastic wrap, and set aside.

Preheat a medium nonstick skillet over medium-low heat. Add the turkey, onion, and jerk seasoning. Cover and cook, occasionally stirring and breaking up the turkey, until no longer pink, about 15 minutes. Remove from the heat to cool.

Scatter the breadcrumbs over a platter or tray. Turn the dough out onto a lightly floured work surface and roll it into a 12 × 9-inch rectangle. With a sharp knife, cut it into 12 (3-inch) squares. Transfer the squares onto the breadcrumbs in batches. Mound 1 tablespoon of the turkey filling in the center of each square and moisten the outer edges with water. With lightly floured fingers, fold each square up over the filling and crimp to secure.

Spray the preheated baking sheet with cooking spray. Put the pastries on the baking sheet and bake for 7 minutes. Spray the pastries with cooking spray, turn them over, and bake for 5 to 6 minutes more, until golden brown all over.

PARMESAN TURKEY

MAKES 6 SERVINGS

PER SERVING
Fat 3 g
Protein 23 g
Carbohydrates 11 g
Calories 170

Goat cheese gives much of the richness associated with considerably higher-fat cheeses, such as triple-crèmes, to this dish. A softer goat cheese, such as creamy Montrachet, can be spread evenly to coat the top of the turkey about halfway through baking if desired, by which time it will have melted sufficiently. For variety, try one of the new flavored nonfat feta cheeses. Whatever other cheese you select, choose a high-quality Parmesan, such as Parmigiano-Reggiano. Inexpensive, pregrated Parmesans tend to be somewhat harsh and loaded with sodium.

Use turkey tenderloin slices. They're the lowest-fat turkey cut available and ready to go from package to pan.

$\frac{1}{2}$ cup Italian-style breadcrumbs (prepared or page 23)

$\frac{1}{4}$ cup grated Parmesan cheese

2 large egg whites

2 tablespoons water

1 pound turkey breast slices

SAUCE

1 teaspoon olive oil

$\frac{1}{2}$ cup chopped white onion

2 cloves garlic, peeled

1 (28-ounce) can crushed tomatoes

3 tablespoons chopped fresh basil

$\frac{1}{4}$ teaspoon ground black pepper

1 (3$\frac{1}{2}$-ounce) package soft goat cheese, crumbled (about $\frac{3}{4}$ cup)

2 tablespoons grated Parmesan cheese

Preheat the oven to 475F (245C). Spray a heavy-gauge nonstick baking sheet with cooking spray.

Mix the breadcrumbs and the ¼ cup Parmesan cheese together on a plate. In a shallow bowl, beat the egg whites and water lightly.

Dip the turkey slices in the egg white mixture and then in the breadcrumb mixture, turning to coat. Place the slices on the prepared baking sheet and spray them lightly. Place the sheet on the bottom rack of the oven and bake for 4 minutes. Turn the slices over and bake for about 3 minutes more, until the turkey is golden on all sides.

Meanwhile, make the sauce. Combine the oil and onion in a large nonstick skillet over medium-high heat. Sauté until the onion begins to brown, about 4 minutes. Press in the garlic and cook, stirring, until it gives off an aroma, 20 to 30 seconds. Stir in the tomatoes, basil, and pepper. Continue to cook until the sauce is very thick, about 5 minutes more.

Spread ¾ cup of the sauce over the bottom of a 13 × 9-inch baking dish. Place the turkey slices over the sauce in a single layer. Spread the remaining sauce over the turkey. Sprinkle the goat cheese over the sauce and scatter the 2 tablespoons Parmesan cheese on top. Bake until heated through and bubbly, about 20 minutes.

CRISPY LEMON QUAIL

MAKES 4 SERVINGS

PER SERVING
Fat 12 g
Protein 20 g
Carbohydrates 12 g
Calories 240

These elegant little birds are rich in iron, phosphorus, potassium, and niacin. Look for them in the freezer cases of gourmet markets, in butcher shops, or in Asian markets. Hot-oven baking seals in juices and yields a succulent bird with none of the dryness that can be associated with quail prepared by other methods. Crispy Lemon Quail goes well with Wild Rice Pancakes (page 196), Vegetable Fried Rice (186), or Griddled Risotto Cakes (page 184). For a traditional presentation, serve it atop risotto cakes cut into wedges to resemble toast points.

2 tablespoons fresh lemon juice

2 tablespoons reduced-sodium soy sauce

2 tablespoons dry sherry

1 teaspoon sesame oil

4 (4-ounce) quail, wings folded under

¼ cup Italian-style breadcrumbs (prepared or page 23)

1 tablespoon chopped fresh parsley

2 teaspoons grated lemon zest

¼ teaspoon ground black pepper

2 tablespoons cornstarch

2 large egg whites

SAUCE

½ cup defatted chicken broth (canned or page 19)

2 tablespoons fresh lemon juice

1 teaspoon cornstarch

½ teaspoon sugar

Combine the lemon juice, soy sauce, sherry, and sesame oil in a medium bowl. Add the quail, toss to coat well, and allow to marinate at room temperature for up to 1 hour.

Place a heavy-gauge nonstick baking sheet in the oven and preheat the oven to 450F (230C).

Combine the breadcrumbs, parsley, lemon zest, and pepper in the bowl of a food processor. Process until finely ground, and transfer the mixture to a plastic bag. Put the cornstarch into a second plastic bag. In a large, shallow bowl, beat the egg whites lightly.

Remove the quail from the marinade and dry them with paper towels. Toss each quail in the cornstarch, shaking off excess. Dip it into the egg whites, and toss to coat in the breadcrumb mixture.

Spray the preheated baking sheet with cooking spray. Lay the quail on their sides on the baking sheet. Bake for 7 minutes. Spray the quail with cooking spray, turn them over, and bake for about 7 minutes more, until the juices run clear when a thigh is pricked with the point of a knife.

Meanwhile, combine all the ingredients for the sauce in a small saucepan over medium-high heat. Cook, stirring occasionally, until clear and slightly thickened, 4 to 5 minutes.

Butterfly each quail by cutting it open along the backbone, turning breast side up, and pushing down to flatten. Drizzle about 2 tablespoons of the sauce over each.

HOT PEPPER WINGS

MAKES 36 WING PIECES

PER PIECE
Fat 3.5 g
Protein 5 g
Carbohydrates 5 g
Calories 70

A great buffet item, these zesty wings boast both hot sauce and cayenne pepper. They're every bit as hot as the Buffalo Anchor Bar's originals, with none of the fat from frying. Lovers of the truly incendiary can boost the hot sauce used to 2 tablespoons and then calm their taste buds with one of our cool buttermilk dressings (see opposite).

In this recipe, we use lots of thick, rich buttermilk, which, contrary to popular misconception, contains no butter and is actually made from cultured skim milk. If you don't have any French bread on hand, use Italian bread or sourdough for the crumbs. You want fresh breadcrumbs rather than the dry commercial variety.

18 chicken wings (about 3 pounds)

2 cups buttermilk

1 tablespoon hot sauce

½ tablespoon garlic powder

1 teaspoon coarse salt

1 teaspoon ground black pepper

½ teaspoon dried thyme

½ tablespoon plus 2 teaspoons dry mustard

1⅓ cups French breadcrumbs (prepared or page 22)

⅔ cup all-purpose flour

1 tablespoon plus 1 teaspoon onion powder

½ teaspoon cayenne pepper

Remove and discard the wing tips. Separate the remaining 2 segments of each wing at the joint.

Combine the chicken, buttermilk, hot sauce, garlic powder, salt, black pepper, thyme, and ½ tablespoon of the mustard in a heavy-duty plastic bag. Squeeze the air from the bag, seal tightly, and shake the bag to coat the chicken evenly. Marinate in the refrigerator for at least 2½ hours or up to 6 hours.

Preheat the oven to 500F (260C). Spray a heavy-gauge nonstick baking sheet to coat lightly with cooking spray.

On a platter or tray, combine the breadcrumbs, flour, onion powder, cayenne, and the remaining 2 teaspoons mustard. Roll the wing pieces in the breadcrumb mixture to coat and let sit for 5 minutes. Roll again, making sure that the chicken is well coated, and let sit for 10 minutes more.

Transfer the wing pieces to the prepared baking sheet. Bake for 15 minutes. Turn wing pieces and bake for 10 to 12 minutes more, until browned, taking care not to let them burn.

DRESSINGS

Try one of these delectable dressings to cool down your Hot Pepper Wings (opposite). Serve with celery sticks on the side.

Blue Cheese Dressing

½ cup reduced-fat mayonnaise

2 tablespoons blue cheese

½ cup buttermilk

¼ cup fresh lemon juice

½ teaspoon Dijon mustard

½ teaspoon salt

¼ teaspoon ground white pepper

MAKES ABOUT
20 TABLESPOONS

PER TABLESPOON
Fat 1 g
Protein 0 g
Carbohydrates 1 g
Calories 15

Mix together the mayonnaise and blue cheese in a small bowl. Stir in the buttermilk, lemon juice, mustard, salt, and pepper.

Mustard Buttermilk Dressing

MAKES ABOUT
16 TABLESPOONS

PER TABLESPOON
Fat 0.5 g
Protein 0 g
Carbohydrates 1 g
Calories 10

½ cup buttermilk

¼ cup reduced-fat mayonnaise

¼ cup fresh lemon juice

½ teaspoon Dijon mustard

½ teaspoon salt

¼ teaspoon ground white pepper

Mix together all ingredients in a small bowl.

Green Goddess Dressing

MAKES ABOUT
20 TABLESPOONS

PER TABLESPOON
Fat 1 g
Protein 0 g
Carbohydrates 1 g
Calories 15

½ cup reduced-fat mayonnaise

½ cup buttermilk

¼ cup tarragon vinegar

2 tablespoons minced fresh parsley

1 tablespoon minced fresh chives

1 tablespoon chopped fresh tarragon

1 clove garlic, crushed

½ teaspoon salt

Mix together all ingredients in a small bowl.

CHICKEN NUGGETS

Marinated in a tequila mixture spiked with green chile hot sauce and boasting a cilantro-flavored coating, these tasty nibbles are a far cry from the fast food snack they may resemble at first glance. For even more kick, you could add up to ½ teaspoon of chili powder to the breading. Serve the nuggets with Tomato Garlic Aïoli (page 251).

MAKES 6 SERVINGS

PER SERVING
Fat 1.5 g
Protein 19 g
Carbohydrates 10 g
Calories 170

¼ cup plus 2 tablespoons tequila

3 tablespoons fresh lime juice

⅛ teaspoon green hot sauce

1 pound skinless, boneless chicken breasts, cut into 1-inch cubes

⅓ cup breadcrumbs

2 tablespoons finely chopped fresh cilantro

⅓ cup all-purpose flour

Preheat the oven to 400F (205C).

Combine the tequila, lime juice, and hot sauce in a large, shallow bowl. Submerge the chicken cubes in the mixture and set aside to marinate at room temperature for about 10 minutes.

Combine the breadcrumbs and cilantro in the bowl of a food processor and process until finely chopped, about 10 seconds. Add the flour and pulse to mix. Transfer the mixture to a plastic bag. Shake the chicken, a few pieces at a time, in the mixture to coat.

Spray a heavy-gauge nonstick baking sheet with cooking spray. Arrange the nuggets on the baking sheet and spray them lightly with cooking spray. Place the baking sheet on the bottom rack of the oven and bake for 7 minutes. Turn the nuggets and bake for about 7 minutes more, until well browned.

PEANUT-COVERED WINGS

MAKES 48 WING PIECES

PER PIECE
Fat 3.5 g
Protein 4 g
Carbohydrates 4 g
Calories 70

These are admittedly an indulgence, what with the peanuts and all, but they really are good. Besides, they're cut into itsy bitsy pieces; let your conscience be your guide. We think these are just about the perfect finger food to serve at a buffet. But be prepared to share your recipe. We hear the wings have been making the cocktail party circuit in Richmond since we whipped up a batch for Deborah Hendricks, Richmond's hostess with the mostest!

Since salted peanuts are used, no additional salt is needed in the recipe.

24 chicken wings (about 4 pounds)

1 cup hoisin sauce

¼ cup reduced-sodium soy sauce

¼ cup dry sherry

1 tablespoon grated fresh ginger

4 cloves garlic, peeled

⅔ cup salted dry-roasted peanuts

1 tablespoon cornstarch

¾ cup all-purpose flour

Remove and discard the wing tips. Separate the remaining 2 segments of each wing at the joint.

Combine the hoisin sauce, soy sauce, sherry, and ginger in a large bowl. Press in the garlic. Add the chicken wings, mix together, and marinate in the refrigerator for at least 1½ hours or up to 6 hours.

Preheat the oven to 450F (230C). Spray a heavy-gauge nonstick baking sheet with cooking spray.

Combine the peanuts and cornstarch in the bowl of a food processor, and process until finely ground. Transfer the contents of the bowl to a plastic bag and add the flour. Shake the wings, a few at a time, in the mixture to coat.

Place the wings on the prepared baking sheet. Spray each wing lightly with cooking spray. Bake for 12 minutes. Spray the wings again, turn them over, and spray the other side. Bake for about 12 minutes more, until golden and crunchy on the outside and cooked through.

BUFFALO GIRLS

MAKES 4 SERVINGS

PER SERVING
Fat 2.5 g
Protein 35 g
Carbohydrates 66 g
Calories 430

For days when there's just not enough meat on those diminutive wings, try this hearty recipe, which brings the same taste sensation to more substantial chicken breasts. Toasted wheat germ is the secret to the nutty coating here; it tastes so good you need not tell anyone just how high in fiber it is, as well as being a concentrated source of vitamins, minerals, and protein. We like the crunch of wheat germ right out of the jar, but you can pulse it a few times in a food processor for a finer consistency.

Serve the Buffalo Girls with Spicy Onion Rings (page 154) or Caribbean Plantain Chips (page 165) and, if desired, some Blue Cheese Dressing (page 85) on the side.

4 (6- to 8-ounce) chicken breasts, bones in

¼ cup unsulfured molasses

2 tablespoons malt vinegar

1 tablespoons plus 1 teaspoon liquid smoke

2 teaspoons garlic powder

1 teaspoon onion powder

1 teaspoon salt

1 teaspoon ground black pepper

½ teaspoon cayenne pepper

½ teaspoon sugar

¾ cup all-purpose flour

¾ cup wheat germ

Remove the skin from the chicken breasts. Combine the molasses, vinegar, liquid smoke, garlic powder, onion powder, salt, black pepper, cayenne, and sugar in a large bowl. Mix thoroughly, add the chicken, turn the breasts to coat well, and set aside to marinate at room temperature for at least 20 minutes.

Place a heavy-gauge nonstick baking sheet in the oven and pre-heat the oven to 475F (245C). Mix the flour and wheat germ together on a plate.

Turn each chicken breast in the flour mixture to coat evenly. Spray the preheated baking sheet with cooking spray. Spray the chicken breasts on both sides and place, bone side up, on the baking sheet. Bake for 20 minutes. Turn the chicken over and bake for 10 to 15 minutes more, until golden on the outside and the juices run clear when pierced.

LIZANNE'S GINGERED DRUMSTICKS

MAKES 6 SERVINGS

PER SERVING
Fat 10 g
Protein 55 g
Carbohydrates 27 g
Calories 450

We created this dish for our friend Lizanne Ceconi, whose motto is "You can never have too much ginger!" When selecting ginger, try to find very fresh baby, or spring, ginger, which is sweet and has a skin so thin and soft it may not need to be peeled, rather than mature ginger with harder, darker skin. Never substitute dried ginger. Serve the drumsticks with Gingered Stir-Fried Vegetables (page 168) and white rice or a simple risotto. You can also fashion the drumsticks into tailored little hors d'oeuvres (see Variation).

If you want to marinate the chicken in a heavy-duty plastic storage bag instead of a baking dish, be sure to push as much air out of the bag as possible before sealing it.

2 cups dry white wine

¼ cup grated fresh ginger

2 large cloves garlic, peeled

1 tablespoon plus ¾ teaspoon five-spice powder (prepared or page 25)

12 chicken drumsticks (about 3 pounds), skin removed

¾ cup cornstarch

2 large egg whites

1 tablespoon water

¼ cup plus 2 tablespoons all-purpose flour

¼ cup plus 2 tablespoons breadcrumbs

¾ teaspoon ground white pepper

Combine the wine, ginger, garlic, and the 1 tablespoon five-spice powder in a shallow baking dish. Mix well and add the drumsticks in a single layer. Cover and marinate in the refrigerator for at least 2 hours or up to 6 hours, turning the drumsticks every hour.

Place a heavy-gauge nonstick baking sheet in the oven and pre-heat the oven to 475F (245C).

Put the cornstarch on a plate. In a large, shallow bowl, lightly beat the egg whites and water. Combine the flour, breadcrumbs, white pepper, and the remaining ¾ teaspoon five-spice powder in a plastic bag.

Dredge the drumsticks in the cornstarch, shaking off any excess. Roll them in the egg white and water mixture, rotating the bowl as needed for even coverage. In batches, shake the legs in the breadcrumb mixture to coat.

Spray the preheated baking sheet with cooking spray. Place the drumsticks on the baking sheet in alternating directions, in a single layer. Spray lightly with cooking spray. Bake for 12 minutes. Turn the drumsticks over, spray them on the other side, and bake for 12 to 14 minutes more, until cooked through and well browned.

Variation: Gingered "Lollipops"

Gingered Lollipops add visual interest to a buffet and are easier to handle when you're trying to eat standing up, balancing a plate and a drink, as is usually the case at a gathering of any size.

To prepare them, sever the skin and tendons attached to the narrow end of each drumstick, using a cleaver or a sharp knife. Gently force the meat down the drumstick toward the thicker end to form a lollipop shape. Scrape the exposed bone clean with a cleaver or knife.

SHELLFISH

WE INITIATED OUR quest to save favorite fried foods from oblivion with many shellfish dishes in mind. Visions of fried shrimp and fritters danced in our heads, along with mouthwatering memories of crab cakes and crawfish scarfed down, spring rolls and soft-shells savored. We believe that nothing strikes longing in the hearts of the nutritionally reformed more than a whiff of the inside of an East Coast crab shack or a Louisiana Cajun roadhouse. Therefore, we set out to re-create the aroma, the crunch, and the flavor of fried shellfish in a manner that everyone could enjoy. Relish these healthy renditions to your heart's delight.

FIERY DUNGENESS CRAB

MAKES 4 SERVINGS

PER SERVING
Fat 3 g
Protein 14 g
Carbohydrates 29 g
Calories 210

CUTTING UP CRAB

Don't be daunted by the sight of a whole Dungeness crab, which is quite a bit easier to clean, trim, and cut than you might suspect. First, remove the apron from the underside of the crab and pry off the top shell. You can save the top shell and batter and bake it, if desired—this is more for dramatic presentation than consumption, since there will be no meat beneath the coating on the shell.

Remove and discard the spongy gills and intestines.

Separate the legs and the pinchers. Cut the body into quarters with a sturdy knife.

It was love at first bite when we first experienced the spicy fried crab at Ho Ho's, a somewhat inelegant, but endearing, eatery in Seattle's international district. We had heard about it from our favorite food writer, who had been sent there by a local of no small culinary repute. We were even more excited a few months later when that same friend escorted us to an obscure storefront restaurant in our own Chicago neighborhood. Hidden on an ambitious Taiwanese menu most of the patrons foolishly overlooked in favor of the Chinese specials of the day, was a superb spicy fried crab!

In this version, we use breadcrumbs to replicate the texture of crab battered and fried in oil, and chili paste with garlic to supply the heat sometimes provided by chopped chiles. The hot-oven baking crisps the shell and makes it snap more easily, revealing all the sweet meat buried inside the crab's many nooks and crannies.

Use the larger and meatier Dungeness crabs from the West Coast rather than blue crabs. Dungeness crabs are sold frozen in gourmet and Asian groceries, and fresh in some fish markets. Fresh or frozen, the highly perishable shellfish will have already been steamed when you buy it.

We often serve the crab family style as the centerpiece of a multicourse dinner. The recipe can easily be doubled if you want to serve it unadorned to a table of crab lovers. Be sure to set out crab crackers, cocktail forks, and bowls for the shells.

1½ cups breadcrumbs

1½ tablespoons garlic powder

1 tablespoon salt

½ tablespoon ground black pepper

¼ cup cornstarch

1 large egg

2 egg whites

2 tablespoons chili paste with garlic

1 (2- to 2½-pound) steamed Dungeness crab, cleaned, trimmed, and cut up (see sidebar opposite)

Place a heavy-gauge nonstick baking sheet in the oven and preheat the oven to 475F (245C).

Combine the breadcrumbs, garlic powder, salt, and black pepper in a plastic bag. Put the cornstarch into a second plastic bag. In a large, shallow bowl, lightly beat the egg, egg whites, and chili paste together.

Two or three pieces at a time, shake the crab legs, pinchers, and body in the cornstarch. Dip them in the egg and chili paste mixture, spooning the liquid into crevices to coat all over, then shake the crab in the breadcrumb mixture.

Spray the preheated baking sheet lightly with cooking spray. Place the pieces of crab on the baking sheet and spray them lightly with cooking spray. Bake for 5 minutes. Turn the pieces over and bake for about 5 minutes more, until the crab is crispy and browned.

CLASSIC MARYLAND CRAB CAKES

MAKES 4 SERVINGS

PER SERVING
Fat 6 g
Protein 30 g
Carbohydrates 17 g
Calories 260

With the possible exception of breakfast, we think crab cakes are perfect for just about every meal. These remind us of the crab cakes sold from stalls in Baltimore's wonderful old downtown food court. We've spared only the fat from frying (just as your kitchen will be spared the veil of fumes from frying oil that permeates the Baltimore complex). Prepared in the original manner, two crab cakes would weigh in at about 20 grams of fat, compared with our 6 grams.

Pair them with a salad of bitter baby greens or mesclun for a satisfying lunch, or with Potato Crisps (page 162) and a green vegetable for a filling dinner. A single crab cake, garnished with a bit of Cayenne Mayonnaise (page 252), makes a generous appetizer. Lay the cake on a bed of French Bread (page 22) and dress with a tomato slice and a few arugula leaves, and you have a fabulous sandwich.

Crush the saltines by hand for a coarse crumb coating, or in a food processor or blender for a finer crumb. Yet another method is to place crackers between sheets of wax paper or seal them in a plastic bag and then crush with a rolling pin. For variety, you can replace half of the crabmeat with ½ cup corn kernels.

1 pound fresh or frozen, thawed crabmeat, cartilage and shell picked out

2 large eggs, lightly beaten

2 egg whites

1 tablespoon fresh lemon juice

1 tablespoon Dijon mustard

4 to 6 drops hot sauce

2 tablespoons chopped fresh parsley

1 tablespoon seafood seasoning (prepared or page 28)

⅛ teaspoon ground black pepper

36 saltine crackers, crushed (about 1 cup)

Combine the crabmeat, eggs, egg whites, lemon juice, mustard, hot sauce, parsley, seafood seasoning, pepper, and ⅔ cup of the cracker crumbs in a large bowl and mix thoroughly. Scoop out a scant ⅓ cup of the crab mixture, roll it into a ball, and then flatten the ball to make a cake. Repeat the process to form 7 more cakes. Put the remaining ⅓ cup cracker crumbs on a plate. Set each crab cake onto the plate, turn it to coat all over, and remove to a clean plate. Cover and refrigerate for about 30 minutes.

Preheat a nonstick griddle or a large nonstick skillet over medium-high heat. Spray the cakes with cooking spray, place them onto the pan, sprayed side down, and cook for 3 minutes. Spray the cakes again, turn them over, and cook until firm and golden, about 3 minutes more. Serve 2 cakes per person.

CRUSTY SOFT-SHELL CRABS

MAKES 4 SERVINGS

PER SERVING
Fat 3 g
Protein 11 g
Carbohydrates 37 g
Calories 220

Frozen, farm-raised soft-shell crabs are now available year-round in many markets, but we still look forward every spring to the start of the fresh soft-shell season, which runs roughly from April to September.

Most plentiful in June and July, soft-shells are Atlantic or Gulf blue crabs that are harvested soon after having shed their hard shells. All too often, they are heavily battered and fried, overseasoned, or sauced with far too much creativity. This presentation is purposely kept simple to highlight the crabs, with which we would recommend just a smidgen of Wasabi Cream (page 262).

For Soft-Shell Crab Sandwiches, serve each crab between slices of French Bread (page 22). Add a little Wasabi Cream and a green of your choice for garnish.

8 (4-ounce) soft-shell crabs, cleaned

1 cup skim milk

4 large cloves garlic, peeled

1 cup breadcrumbs

2 tablespoons fresh parsley

2 teaspoons fresh thyme leaves

2 teaspoons grated lemon zest

½ cup plus 2 tablespoons all-purpose flour

½ teaspoon ground black pepper

1 large egg

2 egg whites

In a very large, shallow bowl, submerge the crabs in the milk in a single layer. Set aside for 20 minutes, turn the crabs over, and allow to sit for 20 minutes more.

Place a heavy-gauge nonstick baking sheet into the oven and preheat the oven to 450F (230C).

Mince the garlic in a food processor. Add the breadcrumbs, parsley, thyme, and lemon zest, and pulse to chop finely. Transfer to a plate. Mix the flour and pepper together on another plate. In a large, shallow bowl, lightly beat the egg and egg whites.

Dredge the crabs in the flour mixture, shaking off any excess. Dip them in the eggs, then turn to coat completely in the breadcrumb mixture.

Spray the preheated baking sheet with cooking spray. Place the crabs on the baking sheet. Bake for 5 minutes, turn them over, and bake for 5 minutes more, until well browned.

CAYENNE POPCORN CALAMARI

MAKES 6 SERVINGS

PER SERVING
Fat 1.5 g
Protein 14 g
Carbohydrates 16 g
Calories 140

Once exotic, calamari has become as popular and all-American as—well, popcorn—in recent years. Here we "fry" it up in very spicy little bits reminiscent of popcorn shrimp. For variety you could substitute miniature shrimp (see page 15–16) for half of the squid. Serve with Tomato Garlic Aïoli (page 251) or Sassy Cocktail Sauce (see opposite).

We serve the calamari as the centerpiece for a Cajun family dinner that would also include Cajun Crab and Corn Beignets (page 104) and a double recipe of Cajun Steak House Potatoes (page 160).

1 pound cleaned calamari (squid), bodies and tentacles

1½ cups buttermilk

1 tablespoon hot sauce

1 cup yellow cornmeal

½ tablespoon cayenne pepper

Cut the calamari bodies into ¼-inch rings. Combine the calamari rings and tentacles, the buttermilk, and the hot sauce in a medium bowl. Cover and marinate in the refrigerator for 1½ to 2 hours.

Place a heavy-gauge nonstick baking sheet into the oven and preheat the oven to 500F (260C).

Combine the cornmeal and cayenne in a plastic bag. Add the calamari, all at once, and shake to coat. Spray the preheated baking sheet to coat lightly with cooking spray. Put the calamari on the baking sheet and spray it lightly with cooking spray.

Bake for 2 minutes. Toss and bake for about 3 minutes more, until well browned.

Sassy Cocktail Sauce

This zesty condiment can perk up Oodles of Oysters (page 122) or Italian-Style Fried Clams (page 118) as well as Cayenne Popcorn Calamari (see opposite).

MAKES ABOUT
7 TABLESPOONS

PER TABLESPOON
Fat 0 g
Protein 0 g
Carbohydrates 4 g
Calories 15

⅓ cup ketchup

¼ teaspoon fresh lemon juice

1 tablespoon prepared horseradish

6 drops hot sauce

Mix all ingredients together in a small bowl.

CAJUN CRAB AND CORN BEIGNETS

MAKES 6 SERVINGS

PER SERVING
Fat 1.5 g
Protein 7 g
Carbohydrates 16 g
Calories 110

This is our savory rendition of a classic French pastry, which we serve as an appetizer on a bed of lettuce, along with a little Pepper Tartar (page 250) or Cherry Tomato Tartar (page 249). Fresh corn is preferable; use frozen in a pinch. Fresh or frozen crab is always preferable to canned. If it's 2:00 in the morning when you decide to whip up a batch, and the realm of the possible includes only canned, make sure it's fancy lump crab and don't tell anyone. We won't.

1 large egg

½ tablespoon Cajun seasoning (prepared or page 24)

1 teaspoon baking powder

½ teaspoon salt

¼ cup skim milk

¾ cup all-purpose flour

4 ounces fresh or frozen thawed crabmeat, cartilage and shell picked out

½ cup corn kernels

2 tablespoons minced green onion (light green and white parts)

Preheat the oven to 450F (230C).

Lightly beat the egg in a medium bowl. Whisk in the Cajun seasoning, baking powder, salt, and milk. Stir in the flour. Fold in the crabmeat, corn, and green onion, combining thoroughly.

Spray a heavy-gauge nonstick baking sheet with cooking spray. Drop the beignets onto the sheet, using about 2 tablespoons of the mixture for each, and spray them lightly on top.

Bake for 7 minutes. Spray the beignets with cooking spray again and bake about 7 minutes more, until golden. Serve 2 beignets per person.

COCONUT PORCUPINE PRAWNS

We call these generously proportioned treats porcupine prawns because of the little bits of coconut in their coating that stick out in all directions. They make a very hefty addition to any buffet, or can be placed atop bitter baby greens and served with a little Mango Lime Salsa (page 259). One per person is quite sufficient! We love the widely available, farm-raised freshwater prawns for their sweetness, but you can substitute colossal shrimp.

MAKES 8 SERVINGS

PER SERVING
Fat 4 g
Protein 13 g
Carbohydrates 17 g
Calories 160

1 cup light coconut milk

1 teaspoon grated fresh ginger

1 teaspoon finely chopped fresh basil

8 large (about 1 pound total) freshwater prawns, peeled and deveined

½ cup all-purpose flour

1 teaspoon red curry paste

⅔ cup sweetened coconut flakes

⅔ cup breadcrumbs

Combine the coconut milk, ginger, and basil in a medium bowl. Toss the prawns in the mixture, cover, and refrigerate for about 2 hours.

Place a heavy-gauge nonstick baking sheet in the oven and preheat the oven to 475F (245C).

Drain ½ cup of the coconut soaking liquid into a shallow bowl. Mix in the flour and curry paste to form a batter. On a plate, combine the coconut flakes and breadcrumbs.

Dip each shrimp into the coconut batter, then roll it in the breadcrumb mixture to coat. Spray the preheated baking sheet with cooking spray, place the shrimp on the baking sheet, and spray them with cooking spray.

Bake for 5 minutes. Turn the shrimp over and bake about 3 minutes more, until well browned.

ROCK SHRIMP SPRING ROLLS

MAKES 4 SERVINGS

PER SERVING
Fat 3 g
Protein 13 g
Carbohydrates 42 g
Calories 250

MAKING MUSHROOM MATCHSTICKS

To cut a button mushroom into matchsticks, first cut the stem flush with the bottom. Position the mushroom, stem side down, on a cutting board and cut vertically into ⅛-inch-thick slices. Stack the slices on their sides and cut crosswise into matchsticks about ⅛ inch thick.

We prefer more delicate Vietnamese spring rolls to the somewhat inelegant, if tasty, egg rolls of Chinese take-out fame. Barry, otherwise known as "Mr. Wizard with a Whisk," has reconfigured the traditional formula for baking rather than frying in oil, thus allowing for shameless overindulgence. One of our favorite appetizers, we think these are particularly good with Apricot Mustard Dipping Sauce (page 255).

If you can't find rock shrimp in your market, substitute 4 ounces medium shrimp, shelled and chopped.

1 teaspoon canola oil

1 cup shredded napa cabbage (about 5 leaves)

½ cup thinly sliced green onions (light green and white parts)

⅔ cup shredded carrot (about 1 carrot)

½ cup thinly sliced celery (about 1 stalk)

½ cup (about 3 large) white button mushroom matchsticks (see sidebar)

2 cloves garlic, chopped

4 ounces rock shrimp, peeled

1 tablespoon reduced-sodium soy sauce

¼ teaspoon sesame oil

¼ teaspoon ground black pepper

8 spring roll or egg roll wrappers (thawed if frozen)

1 large egg white, lightly beaten

Preheat a nonstick stir-fry pan, a large nonstick skillet, or a wok over high heat. Add the canola oil. Add the cabbage, green onions, carrot, celery, mushrooms, and garlic. Stir-fry until the vegetables are wilted and cooked through, about 2 minutes. Add the rock shrimp and stir-fry until they turn opaque, about 1 minute more. Stir in the soy sauce, sesame oil, and pepper. Transfer the mixture to a strainer set atop a bowl to drain and place in the refrigerator until well chilled, about 30 minutes.

Preheat the oven to 400F (205C). Position a wire rack atop a baking sheet.

Spray each wrapper once on top and once on the bottom with cooking spray. Positioning a wrapper as a diamond, mound 3 tablespoons of the chilled filling near the bottom corner. Grasp the tip of the diamond below the mound and fold it up over the filling. Fold the right-hand tip over the filling, then the left-hand tip. Roll the wrapper up so that only the top tip is exposed. Paint the tip with egg white and seal closed. Complete the filling and rolling procedure for the remaining spring rolls.

Place the rolls on the rack atop the baking sheet. Bake about 20 minutes, until golden brown and crispy. Serve 2 spring rolls per person.

BEER-BATTERED CALAMARI

MAKES 8 CALAMARI

PER CALAMARI
Fat 2 g
Protein 11 g
Carbohydrates 14 g
Calories 130

Serve a whole beer-battered calamari per person as an elegant appetizer, atop a bit of mesclun along with a lemon wedge. The flavor of the saltines used in the coating just seems to go with seafood of any type; you could also use ¾ cup oyster cracker crumbs. The crackers and the curry powder that lend this dish its distinctive flavor, when used together, keep each other from clumping. We usually use a pale ale. A darker stout would lend a subtly stronger beer taste to the batter.

8 (about 1 pound total) whole calamari (squid), cleaned

1 cup skim milk

1 cup beer

27 saltine crackers, broken up

¼ cup all-purpose flour

1 tablespoon curry powder

Combine the calamari, milk, and beer in a medium bowl. Cover and marinate in the refrigerator for about 2 hours.

Place a heavy-gauge nonstick baking sheet in the oven and preheat the oven to 500F (260C).

Put the crackers into the bowl of a food processor and pulse a few times to make fine crumbs. (You should have about ¾ cup cracker crumbs.) Transfer the crumbs to a plastic bag and mix in the flour and curry powder. Drain the calamari. In batches, place calamari in the bag and shake to coat well.

Spray the preheated baking sheet with cooking spray, place the calamari on the baking sheet, and spray the calamari with cooking spray. Bake for 3 minutes. Turn the calamari over and bake for 2 to 3 minutes more, until well browned.

Variation: Calamari and Bean Salad

Paired with a navy bean salad, the calamari make a refreshing lunch. Toss 3 cups cooked navy beans with 2 cups torn arugula leaves. For the dressing, mix 1 tablespoon Sun-Dried Tomato Paste (page 117) and ¼ cup water.

On each plate, place about 1¼ cups of the bean mixture atop a bed of mesclun. Top with 2 calamari and drizzle with dressing.

MAKES 4 SERVINGS

PER SERVING (INCLUDING CALAMARI)
Fat 5 g
Protein 33 g
Carbohydrates 59 g
Calories 420

SPICY SHRIMP HUSH PUPPIES

MAKES 8 SERVINGS

PER SERVING
Fat 1.5 g
Protein 8 g
Carbohydrates 16 g
Calories 110

We've gussied up the traditional hush puppy formula a bit in this recipe, including shrimp and bell pepper and substituting masa harina (see page 13), a fine corn flour that produces an outer shell every bit as crisp as fried, for the traditional cornmeal. Serve 2 hush puppies per person as an appetizer, plated with a dollop of Horseradish Cream (page 264), or pile them on a platter for a buffet, with the sauce on the side.

Miniature shrimp, also called salad shrimp, are tiny (about 100 to the pound) shrimp available fresh or canned, in either case precooked. You could also use the diminutive cold-water shrimp of the Pacific Northwest, which are even tinier (about 200 to the pound). Always buy shrimp that smell fresh and briny, not of ammonia.

1 large egg

½ cup skim milk

6 ounces (about 1 cup) cooked, peeled miniature shrimp

1 tablespoon minced green onion

¼ cup chopped green bell pepper

¾ cup all-purpose flour

½ cup masa harina

2 teaspoons Creole seasoning (prepared or page 25)

¾ teaspoon baking powder

½ teaspoon salt

Preheat the oven to 500F (260C).

In a large bowl, whisk the egg and milk together until frothy. Add the shrimp, green onion, and bell pepper. In a small bowl, combine the all-purpose flour, masa harina, Creole seasoning, baking powder, and salt. Slowly stir the dry ingredients into the shrimp mixture.

Drop the hush puppies onto a heavy-gauge nonstick baking sheet, using 2 tablespoons of the mixture for each. Lightly spray them with cooking spray.

Bake until browned, about 5 minutes. Turn the hush puppies over, spray again with cooking spray, and bake 4 to 5 minutes more, until browned on the other side.

CLAM AND PEPPER FRITTERS

MAKES 20 FRITTERS

PER FRITTER
Fat 0.5 g
Protein 2 g
Carbohydrates 5 g
Calories 35

Use any variety of cooked clam you like in this zesty finger food, which is particularly good with a garnish of Cumin Mayonnaise (page 253). See the sidebar for instructions on selecting and shucking fresh clams. If you use canned clams, substitute the liquid in which they are canned for the clam juice, adding a bit of water if needed to equal ¼ cup.

Masa harina is a fine corn flour (finer than cornmeal) that adds a hint of corn flavor to the batter and produces a smoother dough. Look for it in the baking section of your market, or in the Latin section; it is often labeled "for tortillas." The clams and the saltines provide sufficient saltiness that no further salt is necessary.

12 saltine crackers, crushed (about 6 tablespoons)

1 large egg, lightly beaten

¼ cup clam juice

1 teaspoon baking powder

½ teaspoon ground cumin

⅛ teaspoon cayenne pepper

1 tablespoon chopped fresh parsley

½ cup all-purpose flour

¼ cup masa harina

⅔ cup chopped clams

½ cup diced red bell pepper

Place a heavy-gauge nonstick baking sheet in the oven and preheat the oven to 450F (230C). Sprinkle the cracker crumbs over a sheet of wax paper set on a work surface.

In a large bowl, mix together the egg and clam juice. Stir in the baking powder, cumin, and cayenne, then the parsley, flour, and masa harina. Fold in the clams and the bell pepper. Drop 20 fritters

AW, SHUCKS!

You won't be exclaiming "aw, shucks" before the dish is done if you follow a few simple guidelines when selecting and shucking clams—and oysters, for which the same tips apply.

Although mollusks can be purchased almost anytime these days, the old seasonal adage remains true. Clams as well as oysters are at their plumpest and tastiest during those months whose names contain an "r." Select clams or oysters whose shells are tightly closed. If the shells have opened at all by the time you get them home, discard any that do not close again when you tap the shell. Wash and rinse the clams or oysters well in cool water.

To shuck, stick the

by the tablespoonful onto the prepared sheet of wax paper, turning to coat all sides.

Spray the preheated baking sheet to coat lightly with cooking spray. Transfer the fritters to the sheet and spray them lightly with cooking spray.

Bake the fritters for 5 minutes. Turn over and bake for about 5 minutes more, until golden.

point of a small, sharp knife (with a strong blade that won't snap) into the crease where the 2 shell halves meet. Run the knife around to the hinge that joins the shell halves in the back, and rotate the knife blade 90 degrees to pry them open. Pull, then break the shell halves apart at the hinge. With the tip of the knife, sever the muscle that attaches the clam or oyster to the shell. Shuck over a bowl to catch the juice; strain out sand and shell bits before using. And be sure to save the shells for Tammy's Oysters Rockefeller (page 124) or any other recipe that uses them for presentation.

If you initially have trouble prying the clams or oysters open far enough apart to insert the point of a knife, place them in the freezer for 5 to 10 minutes; the cold should force the shell halves apart slightly.

TEQUILA SCALLOPS

MAKES 4 SERVINGS

PER SERVING
Fat 4.5 g
Protein 28 g
Carbohydrates 40 g
Calories 450

Serve these spirited shellfish with rice and Mango Lime Salsa (page 259) as an entree, or with a pitcher of margaritas as an appetizer for 8. We use the large sea scallops both because they are available most of the year and because they are easier to coat and turn for even browning. If you must have the smaller bay scallops when they are in season, shake the pan every 2 minutes while they bake instead of trying to turn this diminutive variety.

Don't worry about the lemon pepper being overwhelming; it is absorbed in the flour sufficiently to tone it down to just the right potency. For variety, substitute a mixture of 2 teaspoons finely grated lime zest and 1 teaspoon ground black pepper for the lemon pepper, and an equal measure of lime zest for the lemon zest in the breadcrumb mixture.

The longer the scallops sit in the tequila, the more pungent and aromatic they become. If desired, marinate for up to 4 hours (cover and refrigerate after 1 hour).

1 pound sea scallops

1 cup tequila

¼ cup all-purpose flour

1 tablespoon lemon pepper

1 large egg

2 egg whites

1½ cups breadcrumbs

¼ cup chopped fresh cilantro

1 tablespoon plus 1 teaspoon finely chopped lemon zest

Lemon or lime wedges

Combine the scallops and the tequila in a medium bowl. Cover and set aside to marinate at room temperature for up to 1 hour.

Place a heavy-gauge nonstick baking sheet in the oven and pre-heat the oven to 450F (230C).

Mix the flour and lemon pepper in a large, shallow bowl. In a second bowl, lightly beat the egg with egg whites. Combine the breadcrumbs, cilantro, and lemon zest in a plastic bag. In batches, coat the scallops first in the flour mixture, then in the eggs. Shake in the breadcrumb mixture to coat.

Spray the preheated baking sheet with cooking spray and place the scallops on the sheet. Bake for 4 minutes. Turn the scallops over and bake for about 3 minutes more, until golden. Serve with wedges of lemon or lime.

SWEET-AND-SOUR SCALLOPS

MAKES 4 SERVINGS

PER SERVING
Fat 2 g
Protein 19 g
Carbohydrates 47 g
Calories 280

This version is most definitely not the radioactive red sweet-and-sour scallops dispensed by your father's favorite Chinese restaurant! Typically, the scallops are deep-fried in oil, then cooked again in the sauce—racking up at least 22 grams of fat and 470 calories along the way. (Prepared with pork rather than scallops in the traditional rendition of this dish, we'd be talking 35 grams of fat and 560 calories.)

We not only pare the fat—down to 2 grams and 280 calories—but save time as well. You don't have to wait for oil to heat up, and the sauce cooks on the stovetop while the scallops are in the oven. And since our scallops are not cooked a second time, in the sauce, they stay crisper than the take-out variety.

Look for the sun-dried tomato paste, which comes in a tube, in your market's Italian section, or make your own (see opposite).

¼ cup cornstarch

¾ cup breadcrumbs

1 large egg white

1 tablespoon reduced-sodium soy sauce

12 ounces sea scallops

SAUCE

1 green bell pepper, cored, seeded, and cut into ¾-inch cubes

1 yellow bell pepper, cored, seeded, and cut into ¾-inch cubes

2 green onions, trimmed to white and light green parts and cut into ⅛-inch rounds

½ cup water

½ cup orange juice

¼ cup rice vinegar

¼ cup packed light brown sugar

2 tablespoons sun-dried tomato paste

Place a heavy-gauge nonstick baking sheet in the oven and preheat the oven to 450F (230C).

Put the cornstarch on a plate and put the breadcrumbs on a second plate. Beat the egg white lightly in a large, shallow bowl and mix in the soy sauce. In batches, dip the scallops into the cornstarch, shaking off any excess, and then into the egg mixture. Roll in the breadcrumbs to coat.

Spray the preheated baking sheet lightly with cooking spray. Put the scallops on the baking sheet and spray them lightly with cooking spray. Bake for 3 minutes. Turn the scallops over and bake about 3 minutes more, until well browned.

Meanwhile, combine all ingredients for the sauce in a medium saucepan and bring to a boil over high heat. Boil until thick and clear, 1 to 2 minutes. Pour about ¾ cup of the sauce over each serving of scallops.

Sun-Dried Tomato Paste

To make about ¼ cup, combine 2 tablespoons coarsely chopped sun-dried tomatoes and ¼ cup plus 2 tablespoons water in a microwave-safe container, cover, and microwave on HIGH power for about 2 minutes, until the liquid is steaming and the tomatoes can be mashed easily. Transfer the mixture to a food processor and process until smooth, about 1 minute. (If the sun-dried tomatoes are very dry and brittle, you may need to drizzle in a little more water.)

ITALIAN-STYLE FRIED CLAMS

MAKES 6 SERVINGS

PER SERVING
Fat 1 g
Protein 8 g
Carbohydrates 21 g
Calories 130

We combine the best of two of our favorite appetizers in this dish—old-fashioned New England fried clams and Italian-accented clams casino. Long, thin razor clams are particularly delectable prepared this way, but since they're hard to find, we recommend the round, meaty cherrystone clams traditionally used in casino preparations. You could also use littlenecks. (The recipe doubles easily, which you will probably want to do if you're lucky enough to encounter some razor clams on your way to the oven.)

Use olive oil spray in this recipe, either commercial olive oil cooking spray or olive oil misted through one of the nifty new oil spritzers now on the market (see page 13). Serve the clams with any tartar sauce; we especially like Cherry Tomato Tartar (page 249) with them.

1 cup Italian-style breadcrumbs (prepared or page 23)

½ cup white cornmeal

2 tablespoons garlic powder

12 cherrystone clams or 24 razor or littleneck clams, cleaned and shucked (see page 112 for shucking directions).

Spray a heavy-gauge nonstick baking sheet with cooking spray and place it in the oven. Preheat the oven to 500F (260C).

Combine the breadcrumbs, cornmeal, and garlic powder in a large, shallow bowl. Add the clams to the mixture, coat, and let sit for 5 minutes.

Transfer the clams to the preheated baking sheet and spray them lightly with cooking spray. Bake for 2 to 3 minutes, until golden. Turn the clams over and bake 2 to 3 minutes more, until golden on the other side.

LOUISIANA CRAWFISH CAKES

Every year we head to the Davis St. Fish Market, our favorite local seafood house, to celebrate the opening of crawfish season, which usually coincides with the start of Mardi Gras. Like many fellow addicts, Kevin just can't get enough of the succulent, often highly spiced, little crustaceans, also called crawdads and mudbugs. Although some Cajuns still maintain their own crawfish ponds, crawfish are no longer exclusively denizens of the bayous. Now commercially farmed to keep us city slickers supplied, they are readily available precleaned and precooked from fish markets and many supermarket seafood counters.

Our healthfully griddled cakes are bursting with corn and crawfish, which are naturally very low in saturated fat. Serve them up with a little Green Tomato Tartar (page 248).

MAKES 4 SERVINGS

PER SERVING
Fat 3 g
Protein 15 g
Carbohydrates 15 g
Calories 150

8 ounces cooked crawfish tail meat

⅔ cup fresh or frozen corn kernels

1 large egg

2 egg whites

¼ teaspoon hot sauce

½ tablespoon Creole seasoning (prepared or page 25)

½ cup Italian-style breadcrumbs (prepared or page 23)

Combine the crawfish and corn in a small bowl. In a medium bowl, lightly beat the egg and egg whites. Whisk in the hot sauce, Creole seasoning, and breadcrumbs. Add the crawfish mixture, and stir to mix thoroughly. Using ¼ cup for each, roll the mixture into 8 balls and then flatten them into cakes. Place on a plate, cover, and refrigerate the cakes for about 20 minutes to firm.

Preheat a nonstick griddle or a large nonstick skillet over high heat. Spray the crawfish cakes lightly with cooking spray and place, sprayed side down, in the pan. Cook until well browned, about 2 minutes per side, spraying the cakes with cooking spray before flipping them over. Serve 2 cakes per person.

KEY WEST SWEET POTATO AND CONCH FRITTERS

MAKES 4 SERVINGS

PER SERVING
Fat 2 g
Protein 31 g
Carbohydrates 37 g
Calories 300

Garnished with a dollop of Cumin Mayonnaise (page 253), these delightful fritters serve 4 as an entree or 6 as a plated appetizer course. Even those who haven't tried the South Florida and island delicacy would likely recognize the colorful shells from which conch (pronounced "konk") come. Although the texture of the high-protein, low-fat conch is rather like abalone, its flavor is closer to that of clam. We use canned conch, which requires no further tenderization. Look in Asian, Caribbean, or Italian groceries if you can't find conch in your supermarket.

4 cups water

2 tablespoons distilled white vinegar

2 medium (about 1 pound total) sweet potatoes, peeled and grated (about 3 cups)

1 (15-ounce) can conch, rinsed, drained, and roughly chopped (about 1½ cups)

¼ cup chopped green onions (trimmed to white and light green parts)

1 large egg, lightly beaten

2 egg whites, lightly beaten

¼ cup plus 2 tablespoons all-purpose flour

¼ cup chopped fresh cilantro

1 teaspoon ground coriander

Combine the water and vinegar in a medium bowl. Add the sweet potatoes and let soak for about 30 minutes. Drain and squeeze dry in paper towels.

Place a heavy-gauge nonstick baking sheet in the oven and preheat the oven to 450F (230C).

In a large bowl, combine the sweet potatoes, conch, green onions, egg, egg whites, flour, cilantro, and coriander. Mix well.

Spray the baking sheet with cooking spray. Drop 12 fritters onto the baking sheet, using about ⅓ cup of the sweet potato and conch mixture for each. Flatten into pancakes with a spatula. Bake for 8 minutes. Spray the fritters with cooking spray and turn them over. Bake for about 8 minutes more, until golden. Serve 3 fritters per person as an entree.

OODLES OF OYSTERS

MAKES 48 OYSTERS

PER OYSTER
Fat 0 g
Protein 1 g
Carbohydrates 3 g
Calories 20

If Kevin could transport himself to another time for a visit, it would undoubtedly be the gastronomically indulgent last turn-of-the-century, when diners feasted on course after course of the likes of vegetable timbales and terrapin stews, roasted game birds and meat pies, and always, always lots of oysters. When we did some work on a Victorian cookbook a few years ago, we tested everything from panned oysters and roasted oysters to pickled oysters and oyster pancakes!

For this healthy rendition of fried oysters, we add a bit of Cajun seasoning, which would have raised a Victorian cook's eyebrows but suits the modern palate perfectly. It's mixed in with delicate semolina flour that does not obscure or overwhelm the naturally briny taste of the oysters. Serve with a little Horse-radish Cream (page 264) on the side. The oysters can be purchased preshucked from your fishmonger. They should be plump, uniform in size, fresh-smelling, and packed in clear liquor. Eastern bluepoints are the most prevalent in many parts of the country, but any variety will do.

¼ cup all-purpose flour

1 cup semolina flour

2 teaspoons Cajun seasoning (prepared or page 24)

2 large egg whites

48 fresh oysters, cleaned and shucked (see page 112) for shucking directions)

Place a heavy-gauge nonstick baking sheet in the oven and preheat the oven to 500F (260C).

Put the all-purpose flour on a plate and combine the semolina flour and Cajun seasoning on a second plate. Lightly beat the egg whites in a large, shallow bowl.

Dredge each oyster in the all-purpose flour, dip it in the egg whites, and roll it in the semolina mixture to coat. Spray the preheated baking sheet to coat lightly with cooking spray, place the oysters on the baking sheet, and spray each oyster lightly with cooking spray.

Bake for about 2 minutes, until the oysters are golden. Turn the oysters over, spray again, and bake for about 1 minute more, until golden brown on the other side.

Variation: Oyster Po'boys

For a special treat, make Oyster Po'boys. Scoop some of the dough out of 2 loaves of French Bread (page 22) to make wells, heap in oysters hot from the oven, add a little Horseradish Cream (page 264) or Cayenne Mayonnaise (page 252), and finish with a bit of torn romaine lettuce. If you're using the Cayenne Mayonnaise, you may wish to add a few thin shavings of fresh horseradish root. Our favorite New Orleans po'boy purveyor (it calls its version a ferdi), the bustling Mother's, adds a bit of "debris," the succulent little browned bits that fall from a roast beef as it cooks.

TAMMY'S OYSTERS ROCKEFELLER

MAKES 48 OYSTERS

PER OYSTER (INCLUDING
FRIED OYSTER)
Fat 2.5 g
Protein 3 g
Carbohydrates 4
Calories 50

When our friend Tammy Blake, who loves good food almost as much as we do, comes to town, the first stop is usually a restaurant. On her last visit we enjoyed a fabulously creative dinner that included venison fajitas, lamb tacos, and an intriguing appetizer that involved fried oysters on the half shell. We took the concept a step farther and created a Rockefeller-like dish that features fried rather than raw oysters, with a touch of cheese. We can't wait to serve it to Tammy!

This recipe is easily halved if you wish to serve the oysters as plated appetizers.

You need 48 oyster half-shells for the recipe, so use oysters in the shell for the fried oysters; see page 112 for instructions on opening oysters.

> 2 (10-ounce) packages fresh spinach, stemmed, rinsed, and drained
>
> 2 tablespoons roughly chopped fresh chives
>
> ½ cup fresh parsley leaves
>
> 2 tablespoons Worcestershire sauce
>
> 48 fried oysters (page 122)
>
> 12 thin slices Muenster cheese, cut into quarters

Preheat the oven to 500F (260C).

In batches, finely chop the spinach, chives, and parsley in a food processor.

Preheat a medium nonstick skillet over medium-high heat. Add the spinach mixture and the Worcestershire sauce. Stirring constantly, cook until heated through and dry, about 2 minutes. Put ½ tablespoon into each of the oyster half-shells. Add a fried oyster to each and top with a piece of cheese.

Place the oyster half-shells on a heavy-gauge nonstick baking sheet. Bake for about 3 minutes, until the cheese has melted, and is bubbly and beginning to brown.

FISH

A PLAIN BROILED fish fillet is indeed a righteous choice nutritionally—and it can taste good drizzled with the right sauce or served alongside a robust vegetable. It's well and good in its place. But it's just not crispy catfish with hush puppies . . . or a griddled salmon cake . . . or a whole fried snapper. Nor is it battered, pan-fried frogs' legs or breaded, deep-fried smelts.

Save the broiled fillet for when somebody's watching, and treat yourself to one of our healthful, "fried" renditions instead. Fish is very low in fat to start with, and we've banned more than a smidgen of oil from the kitchen, so why not indulge in a bit of heavenly crunchy coating?

Cajun Catfish

Breaded Trout Fingers

Monkfish Stir-Fried with Roasted Peppers and Noodles

Smoked Salmon Cakes

Whole Curried Red Snapper

Cornmeal-Coated Catfish Nuggets

Fish Toast Triangles

Salt Cod and Potato Cakes

Tilapia with Green Beans and Water Chestnuts

Japanese Cod Bites

Spicy Smelts

Stir-Fried Asian Frogs' Legs

Buttermilk-Battered Frogs' Legs

CAJUN CATFISH

MAKES 6 SERVINGS

PER SERVING
Fat 4.5 g
Protein 22 g
Carbohydrates 15 g
Calories 200

The day's progress from Chicago to Fort Lauderdale had been an arduous one on a long and dusty highway, and young Kevin and his parents were resigned to a cursory meal and a sound night's sleep when they pulled into the nondescript motel on Route 41 outside Nashville. Interest perked up, however, when the motel's dining room turned out to be a gracefully restored antebellum house hidden on the back of the property. The then otherworldly-sounding catfish turned out to be sweet and juicy beneath a perfectly crisped crust, and the hush puppies were a revelation. The family left with a new appreciation of Southern cooking at its best.

Though long associated with the South and complemented in this recipe by Cajun spices, catfish is farm-raised and widely available these days—fresh in many parts of the country and frozen almost everywhere else. An eminently unattractive fish sporting long, whiskerlike feelers for which it is named, catfish has a surprisingly delicate flavor.

This catfish recipe is our take on the classic, French-inspired preparation favored in Charleston, called crumb-fried. We like to serve it with Green Tomato Tartar (page 248).

    1 cup breadcrumbs

    1 tablespoon paprika

    1 tablespoon Cajun seasoning (prepared or page 24)

    1 teaspoon lemon pepper (prepared or page 27)

    2 large egg whites, lightly beaten

    6 (4-ounce) catfish fillets

    Salt and ground black pepper, to taste

Spray a heavy-gauge nonstick baking sheet lightly with cooking spray. Place it in the oven and preheat the oven to 500F (260C).

Combine the breadcrumbs, paprika, Cajun seasoning, and lemon pepper on a plate. Put the egg whites in a large, shallow bowl.

Dip each catfish fillet into the egg whites, then in the breadcrumb mixture, turning to coat. Place the fillets on the prepared baking sheet and sprinkle with salt and pepper. Bake for 12 to 15 minutes, until the fish is opaque in the center and the topping is browned.

Hush Puppies

MAKES 6 SERVINGS

PER SERVING
Fat 2.5 g
Protein 4 g
Carbohydrates 18 g
Calories 110

Legend has it that the cornmeal fritters called hush puppies were so named for the bits of fried batter tossed to the hounds to keep them quiet during meal preparation in the old South. We like the story, even if it's not true; and we like the namesake dish. Catfish just wouldn't be catfish without the puppies! Whip up a batch and serve 2 per person.

1 large egg

½ cup buttermilk

1¼ cups fresh or frozen thawed corn kernels (about 1 ear)

1 small yellow onion, chopped (about ½ cup)

1 cup all-purpose buttermilk baking mix

½ teaspoon salt

⅛ teaspoon cayenne pepper

Preheat the oven to 500F (260C).

In a large bowl, whisk the egg and buttermilk together until frothy. Add the corn and onion. In a small bowl, combine the baking mix, salt, and cayenne. Slowly stir the dry ingredients into the buttermilk mixture.

Drop the hush puppies onto a heavy-gauge nonstick baking sheet, using 2 tablespoons of the mixture for each. Spray lightly with cooking spray and bake for about 5 minutes, until brown. Spray again, roll the puppies over, and bake 4 to 5 minutes more, until brown on the other side.

BREADED TROUT FINGERS

We were looking for an interesting way to prepare trout when we happened upon this mustard-coated and breaded presentation in a soul food restaurant on Chicago's South Side. (They used catfish, but we kept thinking trout with each bite.)

Use either steelhead or sea trout, both of which are much larger and firmer textured than the smaller brook trout. Steelhead trout is a salmon-colored subspecies of rainbow trout (it's sometimes referred to as salmon trout). Sea trout, also called saltwater trout, is plentiful on the East Coast. It's easy to confuse steelhead and sea trout—even our fishmonger does—but you'll do fine with either of these larger trout varieties.

Serve the trout fingers with Polenta-Encrusted Fried Green Tomatoes (page 170) or Creole Okra (page 177).

½ cup dry white wine

¼ cup Dijon mustard

1 pound steelhead or sea trout fillets, cut into 3 × 1-inch strips

½ cup Italian-style breadcrumbs (prepared or page 23)

2 tablespoons packed fresh parsley

Preheat the oven to 475F (245C). Spray a heavy-gauge nonstick baking sheet lightly with cooking spray.

Combine the wine, mustard, and trout in a medium bowl. Mix to coat.

In the bowl of a food processor, combine the breadcrumbs and parsley. Pulse to chop and incorporate the parsley. Transfer the crumb mixture to a plate.

Dip the trout fingers in the breadcrumb mixture, turning to coat evenly. Place on the prepared baking sheet and spray the trout lightly with cooking spray. Bake for 5 minutes. Turn the trout fingers and bake for about 5 minutes more, until golden brown on the outside and opaque in the center.

MAKES 6 SERVINGS

PER SERVING
Fat 4 g
Protein 14 g
Carbohydrates 8 g
Calories 140

MONKFISH STIR-FRIED WITH ROASTED PEPPERS AND NOODLES

MAKES 4 SERVINGS

PER SERVING
Fat 2 g
Protein 18 g
Carbohydrates 34 g
Calories 260

Brimming with roasted peppers and noodles, this dish makes a hearty meal paired with a loaf of crusty bread, such as French Bread (page 22). Its main component is monkfish, an eminently unattractive fish with a somewhat checkered history and a string of aliases that run the gamut from angelfish to sea devil. Because of its homely exterior, monkfish was long considered a trash fish. Of late, however, more and more cooks have come to appreciate what lies beneath the surface. The meat from the tail portion of the fish, the only edible part, is firm, delicately flavored, and somewhat evocative of scallops in its hint of sweetness.

Look for the cellophane noodles in your supermarket's Asian aisle. Sometimes called bean thread vermicelli, they come dried and need to be soaked in water to plump.

4 ounces cellophane noodles

1½ cups very hot water

1 pound monkfish, cut into 1-inch cubes

2 tablespoons vodka or sake

4 tablespoons reduced-sodium soy sauce

1 teaspoon plus 2 tablespoons cornstarch

¼ cup orange juice

1 cup vegetable broth (canned or page 20)

2 pieces fresh ginger the size of quarters, peeled

6 ounces sweet roasted red bell peppers, cut into thin strips (about ½ cup)

1 bunch red chard, trimmed and chopped (about 4 cups)

2 green onions, trimmed to white and light green parts and cut into rings (about ¼ cup)

Dash of green hot sauce

1 teaspoon grated orange zest

Combine the cellophane noodles and water in a medium bowl. Let soak until soft, about 10 minutes. Meanwhile, combine the monkfish, vodka, 2 tablespoons of the soy sauce, and 1 teaspoon cornstarch in a large bowl. Set aside to marinate while the noodles soak.

In a small bowl, combine the orange juice, ¾ cup of the broth, the remaining 2 tablespoons soy sauce, and the remaining 2 tablespoons cornstarch.

Preheat a nonstick stir-fry pan, a large nonstick skillet, or a wok over high heat. Add the remaining ¼ cup broth and the ginger. Stirring constantly, cook 1 minute. Add the monkfish and its marinade, along with the roasted peppers. Stir-fry until the fish is opaque and the mixture has begun to bubble, about 2 minutes. Remove and discard the ginger.

Add the chard to the pan and stir-fry just until it begins to wilt, about 30 seconds. Drain the noodles and add to the pan. Stir in the orange juice mixture and stir-fry until the chard is completely wilted, about 1 minute. Add the green onions and stir-fry until thick and bubbly, about 30 seconds. Stir in the hot sauce and orange zest.

SMOKED SALMON CAKES

MAKES 6 SERVINGS

PER SERVING
Fat 4 g
Protein 11 g
Carbohydrates 23 g
Calories 170

Served on a bed of radicchio and garnished with lemon wedges and a dollop of sour cream, these cakes make heavenly luncheon fare. Just add a loaf of crusty bread and, if you like, a glass of bone-dry white wine. (For a dinner entree, double the recipe and serve 2 cakes per person.) While the cakes are perfectly fine made with supermarket lox, they will be even better if you splurge a bit and use some Scottish salmon.

Those who normally avoid smoked salmon because it is cold-smoked rather than cooked need not fret about this recipe, as the salmon will emerge from the oven fully cooked. The potato lends an almost velvety texture beneath the crunch of the coating. We prefer the stronger-tasting large Italian capers to the little non-pareils.

4 red potatoes (about 1½ pounds total), peeled and cubed (about 4 cups)

2 tablespoons water

8 ounces smoked salmon, chopped (about 1 cup)

1 large egg

1 tablespoon chopped green onion

1 tablespoon rinsed and drained capers, chopped

1 teaspoon grated lemon zest

¼ cup reduced-fat sour cream

¼ teaspoon salt

¼ teaspoon ground black pepper

9 saltine crackers

1 tablespoon snipped fresh dill

Put the potatoes and water into a microwave-safe container. Cover with plastic wrap and microwave on HIGH for about 5 minutes, until the potatoes are fork-tender. (The potatoes can also be boiled in enough water to cover, for about 20 minutes, on the stovetop.)

Drain the potatoes and put them in a large bowl. Mash the potatoes and allow them to cool to room temperature. Add the salmon, egg, green onion, capers, lemon zest, sour cream, salt, and pepper. Mix well, cover, and refrigerate at least 30 minutes.

Preheat the oven to 475F (245C). Spray a heavy-gauge nonstick baking sheet with cooking spray.

Combine the saltines and dill in the bowl of a food processor, and process until finely ground. (You should have about ¼ cup crumbs.) Transfer the cracker crumbs to a plate.

Form the salmon mixture into 6 cakes, using about ½ cup of the mixture for each. Coat the cakes in the cracker crumb mixture, turning to coat all over.

Place the cakes on the prepared baking sheet and bake for 8 minutes. Spray the cakes with cooking spray, turn them over, and bake for about 8 minutes more, until lightly browned.

WHOLE CURRIED RED SNAPPER

MAKES 4 SERVINGS

PER SERVING
Fat 4.5 g
Protein 14 g
Carbohydrates 22 g
Calories 190

A whole fish never ceases to delight dinner guests; and the wonderfully lean, tasty, hot pink-skinned Atlantic red snapper is one of the greatest crowd pleasers of them all. We've often enjoyed it in Asian, Greek, and fusion restaurants, albeit with quite a bit more fat. For example, Chinese-style whole fried snapper would have about 26 grams of fat and 510 calories. When we prepare this dish, it has only about 4.5 grams of fat and 190 calories.

This recipe has an Indian accent. The spiciness of the curry and ginger marinade, absorbed through the cuts made in the snapper's sides, complements the fish's naturally sweet flavor nicely. Have your fishmonger remove scales, gills, and fins. Hot-oven baking seals in juices. Take care not to overcook; when properly done, the snapper should flake easily and its juices should be milky.

Serve the snapper with Gingered Stir-Fried Vegetables (page 168) and Vegetable Fried Rice (page 186).

1 (1-pound) whole red snapper, ready to cook

1 cup light coconut milk

1 cup skim milk

½ tablespoon red curry paste

½ tablespoon grated fresh ginger

3 tablespoons all-purpose flour

3 tablespoons breadcrumbs

3 tablespoons cornstarch

1 tablespoon white cornmeal

1 tablespoon curry powder

2 teaspoons baking powder

Make 3 diagonal cuts in each side of the snapper. Combine the fish, coconut milk, skim milk, curry paste, and ginger in a heavy-duty plastic storage bag. Squeeze the air from the bag, seal tightly, and set aside to marinate at room temperature for up to 1 hour.

Place a heavy-gauge nonstick baking sheet in the oven and preheat the oven to 450F (230C).

Combine the flour, breadcrumbs, cornstarch, cornmeal, curry powder, and baking powder on a platter or tray. Mix thoroughly. Transfer the snapper to the crumb mixture, and turn to coat all over with the mixture.

Spray the preheated baking sheet with cooking spray and put the fish on the baking sheet. Bake for 7 minutes. Spray the fish with cooking spray, turn it over, and spray the other side. Bake for about 7 minutes more, until the fish flakes easily and is cooked through to the bone.

CORNMEAL-COATED CATFISH NUGGETS

MAKES 6 SERVINGS

PER SERVING
Fat 3 g
Protein 16 g
Carbohydrates 20 g
Calories 170

These tasty morsels work equally well as an appetizer, with a little Cherry Tomato Tartar (page 249), or served up family style as an entree for six, along with Southern Cabbage Slaw (see opposite) and your favorite cornbread. The nuggets sport the cornmeal breading that has become the classic preparation for Southern fried fish over the years. Many supermarket fish counters now carry catfish nuggets, thus saving the work of prepping the fish.

1½ cups buttermilk

1 teaspoon onion powder

2½ tablespoons seafood seasoning (prepared or page 28)

1 pound catfish nuggets or catfish fillets, cut into 1½-inch squares

¾ cup yellow cornmeal

¼ cup all-purpose flour

Combine the buttermilk, onion powder, and ½ tablespoon of the seafood seasoning in a medium bowl. Add the catfish, cover, and marinate in the refrigerator for about 3 hours.

Preheat the oven to 500F (260C). Spray a heavy-gauge nonstick baking sheet with cooking spray.

Combine the cornmeal, flour, and the remaining 2 tablespoons seafood seasoning in a plastic bag. Add the catfish nuggets to the bag, 3 to 4 at a time, shake to coat, and place on the prepared baking sheet.

Bake for 5 minutes. Spray the nuggets with cooking spray, turn them over, and spray again. Bake for about 5 minutes more, until the nuggets are crunchy and golden on the outside and opaque in the center.

Southern Cabbage Slaw

One of the most versatile of side dishes, cabbage slaw makes a good accompaniment to almost any fried food or shellfish entree.

1 tablespoon Dijon mustard

½ tablespoon cider vinegar

⅓ cup reduced-fat mayonnaise

¼ teaspoon green hot sauce

¼ teaspoon sugar

¼ teaspoon salt

2 cups shredded white cabbage

½ cup shredded carrot

¼ cup chopped green onion

¼ cup seeded and chopped green bell pepper

¼ cup seeded and chopped red bell pepper

½ tablespoon celery seed

For the dressing, whisk the mustard and vinegar together in a small bowl. Whisk in the mayonnaise, hot sauce, sugar, and salt.

In a large salad bowl, combine the cabbage, carrot, green onion, bell peppers, and celery seed. Add the dressing and toss to coat well. Serve chilled or at room temperature.

MAKES 6 SERVINGS

PER SERVING
Fat 0 g
Protein 1 g
Carbohydrates 7 g
Calories 30

FISH TOAST TRIANGLES

MAKES 48 TRIANGLES

PER TRIANGLE
Fat 0 g
Protein 1 g
Carbohydrates 3 g
Calories 15

This simple and delightful hors d'oeuvre, if we do say so ourselves, is quick and easy to prepare, extremely low in fat and calories, and all too often overlooked by the home cook. It's our variation on shrimp toast. Mild-tasting catfish is a particularly good foil for the Chinese mustard and cilantro in the marinade (use either a catfish fillet or precut catfish nuggets), but you could easily substitute an equal amount of peeled shrimp or chunked red snapper or perch fillets.

6 ounces catfish fillets, cut into chunks

2 green onions, trimmed to white and light green parts and cut into chunks (about ¼ cup)

1 (8-ounce) can (about ¾ cup) sliced water chestnuts, drained

2 tablespoons chopped fresh cilantro

1 tablespoon dry sherry

1 tablespoon Chinese mustard

1 large egg white

1 tablespoon cornstarch

½ teaspoon salt

¼ teaspoon hot paprika

12 very thin slices white or wheat bread, crusts removed

Combine the catfish, green onions, water chestnuts, cilantro, sherry, mustard, egg white, cornstarch, salt, and paprika in the bowl of a food processor. Process to a smooth paste. (You should have about 1½ cups of the paste.) Cover and refrigerate at least 20 minutes.

Place a heavy-gauge nonstick baking sheet in the oven and preheat the oven to 450F (230C).

Spread about 2 tablespoons of the chilled paste on each slice of bread, covering the bread completely. Quarter the bread slices on the diagonal.

Spray the preheated baking sheet with cooking spray. Place the triangles on the baking sheet. Bake for 5 to 7 minutes, until well browned.

SALT COD AND POTATO CAKES

MAKES 4 SERVINGS

PER SERVING
Fat 3 g
Protein 60 g
Carbohydrates 36 g
Calories 430

Salt cod, *bacalhau* in Portuguese, has been a staple in Mediterranean cuisines ever since Portuguese sailors, who salted and sun-dried the fish at sea, first brought it ashore. Firm and full-flavored, it retains a salty bite even though much of the sodium content is flushed from the fish while it soaks and reconstitutes. It's sold in Italian, Caribbean, and African markets.

The potatoes give these cakes an extremely soft, creamy texture beneath a moderately crisp coating. For a crustier exterior, form the cakes on a sheet of plastic wrap, touching them as lightly as possible with fingertips only, and transfer to the breadcrumb plate and the griddle with a spatula. We like to serve these with Wasabi Cream (page 262) or Tomato Garlic Aïoli (page 251).

12 ounces salt cod, broken into large pieces

3 cold cups water

2 red potatoes (about 12 ounces total), peeled and cut into ¼-inch cubes

½ cup all-purpose flour

½ teaspoon dried thyme

½ teaspoon salt

¼ teaspoon cayenne pepper

1 large egg white

2 tablespoons buttermilk

⅓ cup breadcrumbs

Put the cod in a large bowl. Add enough cold water to cover the cod. Cover the bowl and refrigerate at least 12 hours or up to 36 hours, to allow the cod to reconstitute, changing the water at least once.

Remove the cod to a colander, rinse under cold running water, and drain.

Meanwhile, bring 3 cups cold water to a boil over high heat in a large saucepan. Add the drained cod and the potatoes. Reduce the heat to low, cover, and simmer until the fish flakes easily, 15 to 20 minutes. Drain. Remove any skin or bones from the fish.

Transfer the cod and potatoes to a large bowl and mash them with a large, sturdy fork or a potato masher. Mix in the flour, thyme, salt, and cayenne. Add the egg white and buttermilk and blend with a fork until smooth. Cover and refrigerate for at least 20 minutes.

Place a heavy-gauge nonstick baking sheet in the oven and pre-heat the oven to 500F (260C).

Mound the breadcrumbs on a plate. Form the cod mixture into 8 cakes with lightly floured hands, using about ⅓ cup of the mixture for each. Gently turn cakes in the breadcrumbs to coat evenly.

Spray the preheated baking sheet with cooking spray. Place the cakes on the sheet. Bake for 6 minutes. Spray the cakes with cooking spray, carefully turn them over with a spatula, and bake for about 6 minutes more, until golden, taking care not to burn. Serve 2 cakes per person.

TILAPIA WITH GREEN BEANS AND WATER CHESTNUTS

MAKES 4 SERVINGS

PER SERVING
Fat 3 g
Protein 12 g
Carbohydrates 13 g
Calories 130

An African fish that's been around for centuries—cookbook writer Jean Anderson has reported speculation that it was the fish of the apostle Peter—tilapia is now being farm-raised in the United States. It has a mild, subtly sweet flavor, firm white flesh, and so little fat that it is a regular in our kitchen. In this recipe, we stir-fry it in a complex coconut milk sauce spiked with roasted green chili paste, a Thai condiment that has made its way into mainstream supermarket aisles. Choose light coconut milk, from which much of the fat and calories naturally found in coconut milk has been skimmed. The preparation also works well with catfish and red snapper, as well as with chicken.

Serve the stir-fry on white rice or on the risotto we prepare in the recipe for Griddled Risotto Cakes (page 184).

7 ounces tilapia fillets, cut into ¼-inch cubes

½ cup plus 2 tablespoons light coconut milk

2 tablespoons reduced-sodium soy sauce

1 tablespoon plus 2 teaspoons cornstarch

1 tablespoon roasted green chili paste

¾ cup plus 2 tablespoons defatted chicken broth (canned or page 19)

1½ cups trimmed and roughly chopped green beans

2 pieces fresh ginger about the size of quarters, peeled

1 clove garlic, peeled

1 small yellow onion, cut into thin wedges

⅔ cup canned sliced water chestnuts, drained

Combine the tilapia, 2 tablespoons coconut milk, 1 tablespoon soy sauce, and 1 tablespoon of cornstarch in a medium bowl. Mix and set aside.

In a small bowl, mix together the chili paste and ½ cup chicken broth. Mix in the remaining ½ cup coconut milk, 1 tablespoon soy sauce, and 2 teaspoons cornstarch.

Put the green beans into a microwave-safe container, cover with plastic wrap, and microwave on HIGH for about 1 minute, until lightly cooked but still firm.

Preheat a nonstick stir-fry pan, a large nonstick skillet, or a wok over high heat. Add ¼ cup of the broth, the ginger, and garlic. Stirring constantly, cook 1 minute. Add the onion and stir-fry for 1 minute. Add the water chestnuts and stir-fry until browned, about 30 seconds. Add the green beans and stir-fry for 30 seconds more. Transfer the contents of the pan to a bowl, discarding the ginger and garlic.

Add the remaining 2 tablespoons broth and the tilapia to the pan. Cook, stirring, until the tilapia has turned completely opaque, about 2 minutes. Add the chili paste mixture and stir-fry until thickened, 1 minute. Return the green beans, water chestnuts, and onion to the pan. Stir-fry to combine and heat through, about 30 seconds.

JAPANESE COD BITES

MAKES 4 SERVINGS

PER SERVING
Fat 2 g
Protein 22 g
Carbohydrates 15 g
Calories 190

There used to be a wonderful Japanese hotel in Chicago with a sake bar tucked away in its basement. In addition to a selection of sakes that was eye-opening to the novice taster, the bar served up little plates of appetizers, rather like Japanese tapas, from the grill around which it was built. We like to serve these scrumptious morsels in similar fashion, on lacquered trays with chopsticks, accompanied by rice, Pickled Ginger (see opposite), and sake.

Sake is a rice wine with a fairly low alcohol content. It is often served warm, although the best sakes, the equivalent of single-malt scotches, are served chilled. We usually cook with a better quality sake than would really be needed, in order to be able to enjoy the rest of the bottle on the side.

½ cup sake

½ tablespoon grated fresh ginger

1 pound cod fillets, cut into 1-inch chunks

½ cup oyster crackers

2 tablespoons fresh parsley leaves

⅓ cup all-purpose flour

Preheat the oven to 400F (205C).

Combine the sake, ginger, and cod in a medium bowl. Set aside to marinate at room temperature for about 20 minutes.

Combine the oyster crackers and parsley in the bowl of a food processor and process until finely ground, about 10 seconds. Add the flour and pulse to mix. Transfer the mixture to a plastic bag. Drain the cod, add to the crumb mixture, and shake to coat.

Spray a heavy-gauge nonstick baking sheet with cooking oil spray. Put the cod on the sheet and spray lightly with cooking spray. Bake for 7 minutes. Spray the cod, turn over, and bake 6 to 8 minutes more, until well browned.

Pickled Ginger

As Lizanne of Lizanne's Gingered Drumsticks fame (page 92) would say, "You really can't ever have too much ginger!" We pickle our own at home to serve with Japanese Cod Bites. We recommend using a mandoline to slice the ginger paper-thin. This recipe will yield not only terrific pickled ginger, just like what you get in a sushi bar, but also an intriguing gingered vinegar (the steeping liquid) that can be used in any of your favorite vinaigrette recipes.

6 ounces fresh ginger, peeled and very thinly sliced (about ¾ cup)

1 cup rice vinegar

¼ cup distilled white vinegar

¼ cup plus 2 tablespoons sugar

1 tablespoon coarse salt

Bring 2 cups of water to a boil in a medium saucepan. Remove from the heat and add the fresh ginger, making sure the water covers it, and let stand 5 minutes. Drain and transfer the ginger to a clean 1-pint (2-cup) glass jar or plastic storage container.

In a microwave-safe container, combine the vinegars, sugar, and salt. Microwave on HIGH about 3 minutes, until the mixture is clear and the sugar is dissolved, stirring about halfway through.

Pour the mixture over the ginger, seal, and allow to steep overnight in the refrigerator before using.

MAKES ABOUT
12 TABLESPOONS

PER TABLESPOON
Fat 0 g
Protein 0 g
Carbohydrates 7 g
Calories 30

SPICY SMELTS

MAKES 4 SERVINGS

PER SERVING
Fat 4 g
Protein 25 g
Carbohydrates 12 g
Calories 190

From the kitchen windows of our Chicago high-rise, you can see a few miles down the Lake Michigan shore to a fishing pier that is the center of activity for our city's brief, frenzied smelting season. During that time the lakefront is as inundated with avid smelters as the lake is with the small, silvery fish. Reputedly best as fresh as possible, the smelts are eaten right out of the lake by fishermen who cook them over bonfires built in sturdy metal trash cans the city fathers wisely haul in for the occasion. Tiny and tender, smelts require no prepping; they can be eaten whole, delicate bones and all.

Far from being a Lake Michigan exclusive, smelts are found on both coasts as well as in the other Great Lakes. The Pacific Coast variety is also called candlefish, because Indians would dry and make candles out of them. In most places, they are available fresh from September to May. For no reason we can readily fathom, the season in Chicago is March to June. They're flash-frozen, however, and therefore available year round in most of the country.

Kevin used to fry up bunches of smelts in oil every year, a practice no longer looked upon with favor by many dinner guests—small wonder, since his recipe produced about 21 grams of fat and 390 calories per serving. Hence our healthier rendition, which boasts only 4 grams of fat and 190 calories per serving. It serves eight as a plated appetizer along with a little Pepper Tartar (page 250). As a main course, serve the smelts with Spicy Onion Rings (page 154) and Southern Cabbage Slaw (page 137).

½ cup all-purpose flour

½ teaspoon lemon pepper (prepared or page 27)

¾ cup yellow cornmeal

2 tablespoons seafood seasoning (prepared or page 28)

1 large egg

2 egg whites

1 pound large smelts (about 24)

Place a heavy-gauge nonstick baking sheet in the oven and preheat the oven to 475F (245C).

Combine the flour and lemon pepper in a plastic bag, and the cornmeal and seafood seasoning in a second bag. Combine the egg and egg whites in a large, shallow bowl, and beat lightly.

In batches, shake the smelts in the flour mixture to coat, then shake off excess flour. Dip each into the egg mixture. A few at a time, shake the smelts in the cornmeal mixture to coat.

Spray the preheated baking sheet lightly with cooking spray. Place the smelts on the sheet and spray again to coat them lightly. Bake for 5 minutes, turn the smelts over, and bake for about 5 minutes more, until very crispy and golden brown.

STIR-FRIED ASIAN FROGS' LEGS

MAKES 4 SERVINGS

PER SERVING
Fat 1 g
Protein 41 g
Carbohydrates 12 g
Calories 230

Plump, tender, and sweet, frogs' legs are one of our favorite foods. Naturally low in fat and calories (less fat and about half the calories of chicken legs), they are farm-raised and sold fully dressed and ready to cook. Frogs' legs are now readily available frozen in most parts of the country. They're even better fresh, if you can find them—check gourmet markets during the spring and summer. Select legs that are pale pink, and take care not to over-cook them. As is the case with most fish, frogs' legs tend to toughen rather than become tenderer the longer they are cooked.

This quick stir-fry is something of an Asian version of a Provençal preparation, brimming with garlic, onion, tomatoes, and mushrooms. We like it with Vegetable Fried Rice (page 186).

2 pounds frogs' legs (about 10 pairs), separated

2 tablespoons dry sherry

¼ cup plus 2 tablespoons reduced-sodium soy sauce

2 teaspoons plus 1 tablespoon cornstarch

¾ cup defatted chicken broth (canned or page 19)

2 teaspoons grated fresh ginger plus 1 strip ginger about 2 × 1 × ¼-inch, peeled

2 cloves garlic, peeled

1 large yellow onion, thinly sliced lengthwise

3½ ounces shiitake mushrooms, cleaned, stemmed, and sliced

2 plum tomatoes, quartered

Combine the frogs' legs, sherry, ¼ cup of soy sauce, and 2 teaspoons of cornstarch in a medium bowl. Cover and marinate in the refrigerator for at least 20 minutes and not more than 2 hours.

For the sauce, combine ½ cup of the chicken broth, the remaining 2 tablespoons soy sauce, the remaining 1 tablespoon cornstarch, and the grated ginger in a small bowl. Press in 1 clove of garlic. Mix well and set aside.

Preheat a nonstick stir-fry pan, a large nonstick skillet, or a wok over high heat. Add the remaining ¼ cup chicken broth, the strip of ginger, and the remaining clove of garlic. Heat just until the broth is sizzling. Add the onion and mushrooms, and stir-fry until the onion is beginning to brown, about 1½ minutes. Add the tomatoes and cook until they begin to soften and give off liquid, about 30 seconds. Transfer the vegetables to a bowl. Remove and discard the ginger and garlic.

Add the frogs' legs to the pan, discarding the marinade. Stir-fry until they start to brown, about 2 minutes. Stir in the sauce. Stir-fry until the sauce starts to thicken. Return the vegetables to the pan. Reduce the heat to medium and cook until the legs are cooked through (opaque at the bone), 4 to 5 minutes more, stirring for the first 2 to 3 minutes.

BUTTERMILK-BATTERED FROGS' LEGS

MAKES 4 SERVINGS

PER SERVING
Fat 4.5 g
Protein 42 g
Carbohydrates 24 g
Calories 320

Frogs' legs are an object of worship at Phil Smidt's, a seafood temple nestled in a gritty Indiana steel mill community about an hour's drive around the lake from Chicago. Yes, they will serve you perch as well, but people have been making the trek to Smidt's for generations for only one reason—the frogs' legs. They're lightly battered, accompanied by a relish assortment the likes of which you haven't seen anywhere else in decades, and served up by an army of veteran waitresses in a series of pink-accented dining rooms.

Our take on Phil's favorite will come out of the oven crunchier if you let the legs sit on a cooling rack for a few minutes between breading and baking. We like to serve this delicacy, which does, as the saying goes, taste somewhat like chicken with a medley of tartar sauces. Use Green Tomato Tartar (page 248), Pepper Tartar (page 250), Cherry Tomato Tartar (page 249), or a plain tartar mixture made with 1 tablespoon pickle relish for every 3 tablespoons mayonnaise.

2 cups buttermilk

1 tablespoon paprika

2 pounds frogs' legs (about 10 pairs), separated

36 saltine crackers, crushed (about 1 cup crumbs)

2 tablespoons lemon pepper (prepared or page 27)

Mix the buttermilk and paprika together in a medium bowl. Add the frogs' legs, cover, and marinate in the refrigerator for about 2 hours.

Combine the cracker crumbs and lemon pepper in a plastic bag. One leg at a time, shake the frogs' legs in the crumb mixture to coat. Lay the coated legs on a cooling rack and set aside for 10 to 15 minutes.

Meanwhile, place a heavy-gauge nonstick baking sheet in the oven and preheat the oven to 500F (260C).

Spray the preheated baking sheet with cooking spray, place the legs on the sheet, and spray the legs. Bake for 5 minutes, turn the legs over, and bake for about 5 minutes more, until golden.

VEGETABLES

FROM CLASSIC COUNTRY fixin's like fried green tomatoes and okra to the French fries and onion rings we nibble alongside the sandwiches and take-out fare that comprise many a meal in today's harried world, we do love our veggies fried. Crusty hash browns can perk up breakfast as much as crisp on the outside, fluffy inside steak house potatoes can dinner. And potato pancakes are a treat any time of the day.

Obviously, we took it to heart when mom said that we should eat vegetables because they are good for us—even if some of the incarnations in which we came to enjoy them were not quite what she had in mind. Mom, however, would be proud of our healthy deep-fry alternatives for everybody's favorite fried foods. She'd be thrilled that we're getting reacquainted with the likes of squash, eggplant, and broccoli even as we explore ways to prepare beta carotene-rich sweet potatoes and invent low-fat renditions of popular snack chips.

Spicy Onion Rings

Curried Sweet Potato Fries

Vinegar and Salt French Fries

Spicy Sweet Potato Chips

Cajun Steak House Potatoes

Barbecue Chips

Potato Crisps

Good, Old-Fashioned Hash Browns

Good, New-Fangled Hash Brown Salad

Caribbean Plantain Chips

Blue Corn–Coated Plantain Coins

Gingered Stir-Fried Vegetables

Polenta-Encrusted Fried Green Tomatoes

Summer Vegetable Hash

Eggplant Panini

Jill's Crispy Zucchini Rounds

Creole Okra

Chive Potato Pancakes

SPICY ONION RINGS

MAKES 4 SERVINGS

PER SERVING
Fat 3 g
Protein 8 g
Carbohydrates 35 g
Calories 200

Kevin pretty much reformed his eating habits with the simultaneous onset of middle age and publication of our first fat-free cookbook. Onion rings, however, were long the exception. Until we developed this guilt-free rendition, they were the smoking gun in an otherwise blameless diet. These rings are first dipped in an egg white mixture, then dredged in a combination of breadcrumbs and cornmeal. While they bake, the egg white hardens to a firm shell; the breadcrumbs and cornmeal give the crusty texture for which we love onion rings. Chili powder provides an unexpected accent.

2 medium (about 1 pound total) white onions

4 large egg whites, lightly beaten

½ tablespoon canola oil

¼ cup all-purpose flour

2 teaspoons chili powder

Salt and ground black pepper, to taste

1 cup breadcrumbs

1 cup yellow cornmeal

Preheat the oven to 425F (220C). Coat a heavy-gauge nonstick baking sheet lightly with cooking spray. Cut the onions into ¼-inch slices and separate into rings.

Combine the egg whites, oil, flour, chili powder, salt, and pepper in a large shallow bowl, and whisk to blend. On a plate, combine the breadcrumbs and cornmeal.

Submerge each ring in the egg white mixture, then in the breadcrumbs and cornmeal to coat. Place on the prepared baking sheet. Spray each onion ring twice with cooking spray. Bake for 10 minutes. Turn the rings, spray each onion ring twice with cooking spray, and bake until browned, about 5 minutes more.

CURRIED SWEET POTATO FRIES

Now that we have all heard about the cancer-inhibiting propensities of beta-carotene, sweet potatoes, which abound in it, are beginning to become as popular elsewhere as they have long been in the American South. Confusion abounds about the different varieties of sweet potatoes, heightened by the mislabeling of them as yams, a term that means something quite different to much of the world. This recipe will take on a range of flavor gradations depending upon the strength of the curry powder you use.

If you have a mandoline, the matchsticks can easily be cut with the French fry disk. The recipe will serve 8 as a snack.

2 to 3 sweet potatoes (about 1½ pounds total)

1 tablespoon canola oil

2 teaspoons curry powder (prepared or page 26)

Preheat the oven to 500F (260C). Spray a heavy-gauge nonstick baking sheet with cooking spray.

Peel the sweet potatoes. Slice crosswise into ¼-inch rounds, and then cut each round into ¼-inch matchsticks.

Combine the sweet potato matchsticks, oil, and curry powder in a large bowl. Toss to coat and transfer the matchsticks to the prepared baking sheet. Bake for 10 minutes. Turn the fries over and bake for about 10 minutes more, until golden.

MAKES 6 SERVINGS

PER SERVING
Fat 2.5 g
Protein 2 g
Carbohydrates 28 g
Calories 140

VINEGAR AND SALT FRENCH FRIES

MAKE 4 SERVINGS

PER SERVING
Fat 3.5 g
Protein 2 g
Carbohydrates 17 g
Calories 100

These are the very crispy sort of fries that generally appeal to adults and would do justice to the perfectly cooked steak you might want to indulge in, given all the fat grams you're saving through healthy frying. The potatoes are first soaked in a water and vinegar mixture to draw out starch and firm them up, then tossed in just a smidgen of oil to facilitate even oven browning. After baking, the matchsticks are tossed in a little vinegar to flavor and coat so that salt will adhere.

Our fries have only 3.5 grams of fat and 100 calories per serving, compared with McDonald's 17 grams of fat and 320 calories!

2 (about $1\frac{1}{4}$ pounds total) baking potatoes, peeled

3 cups water

2 tablespoons plus 2 teaspoons distilled white vinegar

1 tablespoon canola oil

Salt to taste

Cut the potatoes lengthwise into $\frac{1}{4}$-inch slices, then crosswise into matchsticks. Combine the water and the 2 tablespoons vinegar in a large bowl. Completely submerge the potato matchsticks in the mixture and allow to soak for 30 minutes.

Preheat the oven to 400F (205C).

Drain the potatoes on paper towels. Transfer to a clean, dry bowl and toss with the oil. Arrange the potatoes on a heavy-gauge nonstick baking sheet in a single layer. Bake until the potatoes are just beginning to brown, about 20 minutes. Turn and bake about 10 minutes more, until completely browned and crisped.

Remove from the oven and toss with the remaining 2 teaspoons vinegar and the salt.

How could you possibly serve fries without ketchup? Here are a few of our favorites, conjured up quickly by doctoring tomato ketchup.

Hot and Spicy Ketchup

½ cup ketchup

2 tablespoons chopped fresh cilantro

2 teaspoons seeded and chopped jalapeño chile

½ teaspoon salt

**MAKES ABOUT
10 TABLESPOONS**

PER TABLESPOON
Fat 0 g
Protein 0 g
Carbohydrates 3 g
Calories 15

Mix together all ingredients in a small bowl.

Basic Basil Ketchup

½ cup ketchup

¼ cup chopped fresh basil

1 teaspoon fresh lime juice

½ teaspoon ground black pepper

**MAKES ABOUT
12 TABLESPOONS**

PER TABLESPOON
Fat 0 g
Protein 0 g
Carbohydrates 3 g
Calories 15

Mix together all ingredients in a small bowl.

Sweet and Sassy Ketchup

½ cup ketchup

2 teaspoons rice vinegar

1 tablespoon dry mustard

2 teaspoons granulated light brown sugar

2 teaspoons finely diced candied ginger

**MAKES ABOUT
12 TABLESPOONS**

PER TABLESPOON
Fat 0 g
Protein 0 g
Carbohydrates 4 g
Calories 20

Mix together all ingredients in a small bowl

SPICY SWEET POTATO CHIPS

MAKES 6 SERVINGS
PER SERVING
Fat 2.5 g
Protein 1 g
Carbohydrates 21 g
Calories 110

This is our homemade version of those spiffy new vegetable chips that are edging potato chips off the shelves in gourmet markets. (We had to come up with our own when we read the fine print and learned that our favorite, the sweet potato chips, came with over 5 grams of fat in every 1-ounce serving!) The sweet potatoes in this recipe are baked longer at a lower temperature than are those in our Curried Sweet Potato Fries (page 155), yielding a drier and crisper dish that can serve as either a snack or an hors d'oeuvre.

The addition of the sugar was suggested by a similar snack item served by a local microbrewery. (And, yes, the chips do go well with beer.) It nicely counters the salty spiciness of the cayenne and celery salt.

1 tablespoon sugar

1 teaspoon celery salt

⅛ teaspoon cayenne pepper

2 medium sweet potatoes (about 1 pound total)

1 tablespoon canola oil

Preheat the oven to 300F (150C). Spray a heavy-gauge nonstick baking sheet with cooking spray. Mix together the sugar, celery salt, and cayenne in a small bowl.

Peel and very thinly slice the sweet potatoes. Toss them with the oil in a medium bowl. Arrange the slices in a single layer on the prepared baking sheet.

Bake for 5 minutes. Sprinkle with half of the seasoning mixture and bake for 5 minutes more. Turn the potato slices, sprinkle with the remaining seasoning mixture, and bake for another 5 minutes. Remove any chips that have already browned. Turn and move to the outer edges of the pan any chips that look undercooked. Bake 5 to 6 minutes more, until all chips are browned, taking care not to burn them.

Cook's Tip: Instead of buying prepared celery salt, you can make your own fresh celery salt by combing 2 tablespoons celery seed with ¼ cup coarse salt and processing to a fine grind in a spice grinder, coffee grinder, or mini food processor.

CAJUN STEAK HOUSE POTATOES

MAKES 4 SERVINGS

PER SERVING
Fat 1.5 g
Protein 2 g
Carbohydrates 18 g
Calories 90

These thick, steak house–cut potatoes are assertive enough to stand up to the likes of dishes as robust as Cajun Catfish (page 126), but can also add life to a range of plain grilled entrées, from seafood to steak. Unlike uniformly crisp French fries, steak house potatoes have a soft center beneath a crisp outer shell.

2 large (about 1½ pounds total) baking potatoes

1 teaspoon canola oil

2 teaspoons paprika

½ teaspoon salt

½ teaspoon Cajun seasoning (prepared or page 24)

Preheat the oven to 450F (230C).

Cut each potato lengthwise into 8 spears. Rub the spears with canola oil to coat lightly and place in a plastic bag. Add the paprika, salt, and Cajun seasoning. Shake to coat.

Place the potato spears on a heavy-gauge nonstick baking sheet. Bake for about 25 minutes, until they are fork-tender.

BARBECUE CHIPS

You can indulge in this zesty snack with none of the guilt associated with high-fat, high-sodium commercial snack chips. Be sure to slice the potato very thin and soak them for the full 2 hours to firm. Slicing is accomplished most easily by using a mandoline, a contraption that is fitted with slicing disks that make delicate preparation of all sorts of vegetables a snap. Some steel mandolines are pricey, but you can find inexpensive plastic models at kitchenware stores that are worth every penny for avoiding nicked fingers, mangled veggies, and frazzled nerves!

MAKES 6 SERVINGS

PER SERVING
Fat 0 g
Protein 1 g
Carbohydrates 13 g
Calories 60

1 large baking potato (about 12 ounces)

3 cups water

3 tablespoons distilled white vinegar

½ tablespoon sugar

¾ teaspoon barbecue seasoning

¾ teaspoon salt

Thinly slice the potato. Combine with the water and vinegar in a medium bowl, and allow to soak for about 2 hours.

Preheat the oven to 350F (175C). Mix the sugar, barbecue seasoning, and salt together in a small bowl.

Drain the potato slices and pat them thoroughly dry with paper towels. Spray a heavy-gauge nonstick baking sheet with cooking spray and arrange the slices on it in a single layer. Bake for 7 minutes. Spray the chips with cooking spray, sprinkle with half of the seasoning mixture, turn them over, and sprinkle with the remaining seasoning. Bake for about 10 minutes more, until the chips are crisped, curled, and browned. Remove from the oven and let cool on the baking sheet.

POTATO CRISPS

MAKES 4 SERVINGS

PER SERVING
Fat 2.5 g
Protein 2 g
Carbohydrates 18 g
Calories 100

Soaking potatoes in water will draw out some starch (however, not as much as soaking them in a water and vinegar mixture would). Here the result is a texture more like that of what are often called American fries than that of a chip—better suited to serving as a side dish than as a snack.

The crisps are particularly good with Chicken Nuggets (page 87).

2 (about 1 pound total) red potatoes

3 cups cold water

2 teaspoons canola oil

½ tablespoon seafood seasoning (prepared or page 28)

Peel and very thinly slice the potatoes. Put them into a large bowl and soak in the water for about 20 minutes.

Preheat the oven to 375F (190C).

Drain the potatoes, pat them dry with paper towels, and toss with the oil. Arrange in a single layer on a heavy-gauge nonstick baking sheet. Bake for 5 minutes. Turn the slices over and bake for another 5 minutes. Dust the potatoes with ¼ teaspoon of the seafood seasoning and turn them over. Dust the other side with the remaining seasoning and bake for about 5 minutes more, until golden brown and crisp.

GOOD, OLD-FASHIONED HASH BROWNS

Old-fashioned hash browns are the perfect accompaniment for just about anything. We thinly slice the potatoes for extra crispness, but they could also be cut into ½-inch cubes. If you use cubes, shake the baking sheet every 10 minutes or so while the potatoes bake, rather than turning them midway through.

MAKES 6 SERVINGS

PER SERVING
Fat 1.5 g
Protein 1 g
Carbohydrates 15 g
Calories 80

1 pound new red potatoes, sliced

1 tablespoon water

2 teaspoons canola oil

Salt, to taste

Ground black pepper, to taste

Preheat the oven to 350F (175C).

Put the sliced potatoes and water in a shallow, microwave-safe container. Cover with plastic wrap and microwave on HIGH power until the potatoes are fork-tender, 3 to 5 minutes. Toss with the oil and place in a single layer on a heavy-gauge nonstick baking sheet.

Bake for 15 minutes. Turn the slices over and bake for about 15 minutes more, until very crisp and well browned. Season generously with salt and pepper.

GOOD, NEW-FANGLED HASH BROWN SALAD

MAKES 6 SERVINGS

PER SERVING (INCLUDING
HASH BROWNS)
Fat 5 g
Protein 2 g
Carbohydrates 20 g
Calories 140

No bacon drippings in sight in this healthy rendition, although we do indulge in 2 slices of turkey bacon. Bake the bacon in the oven simultaneously with the potatoes for about 20 minutes. Enjoy the luscious warm vinaigrette entrée salad that can be made with the Good, Old-Fashioned Hash Browns.

8 ounces cherry tomatoes, halved

½ cup diced red onion

¼ cup chopped fresh parsley

2 teaspoons finely chopped fresh rosemary

½ cup reduced-fat mayonnaise

1 teaspoon Dijon mustard

¼ teaspoon ground black pepper

2 strips turkey bacon, cooked and diced

½ teaspoon mustard seed

¼ cup cider vinegar

1 recipe Good, Old-Fashioned Hash Browns (page 163)

Combine the tomatoes, onion, parsley, and rosemary in a large bowl. Add the mayonnaise, mustard, pepper, and bacon. Mix well and set aside.

Put the mustard seed into a medium skillet. Cover and cook over medium-high heat, shaking the pan, until the seeds begin to pop. Remove from the heat, add the vinegar, and re-cover. When all the mustard seeds have popped, add the contents of the pan to the tomato mixture in the bowl. Add the potatoes and toss to coat.

CARIBBEAN PLANTAIN CHIPS

A larger, firmer relative of the banana (indeed, sometimes called a "vegetable banana"), the plantain can be found throughout the tropics and is a staple in Latin America, where it is used much as North Americans use potatoes. As they ripen and sweeten, plantains progress in color from green to yellow to almost black. For these savory snack chips, choose a green plantain firm enough to be sliced very thin.

We sprinkle these chips with adobo, a popular Caribbean seasoning that takes on a slightly different character on every island. Puerto Rican cooks shake the dry seasoning mixture onto meat and seafood, while the Cubans add liquid to make it into a rub. Serve the chips with Mixed Pepper Salsa (page 260).

1 (about 10 ounces) green plantain

1 cup water

1 teaspoon distilled white vinegar

½ teaspoon adobo seasoning (prepared or page 23)

Peel the plantain and slice it very thin on the diagonal. Combine in a small bowl with the water and vinegar. Let soak for about 1 hour.

Preheat the oven to 350F (175C). Spray a heavy-gauge nonstick baking sheet with cooking spray.

Drain the plantain slices and pat them dry with paper towels. Lay the slices on the prepared baking sheet and spray them lightly with cooking spray. Bake for 5 minutes. Turn the slices over and bake for 5 minutes more. Move any chips that have begun to curl to the center of the sheet. Sprinkle the chips with the adobo seasoning and bake 4 to 5 minutes more, until golden and crisp.

MAKES 6 SERVINGS

PER SERVING
Fat 0 g
Protein 0 g
Carbohydrates 10 g
Calories 35

BLUE CORN-COATED PLANTAIN COINS

MAKES 4 SERVINGS

PER SERVING
Fat 0.5 g
Protein 2 g
Carbohydrates 25 g
Calories 100

Plantains are what one nutritionist calls a "stellar source" of beta-carotene, to say nothing of their generous helpings of potassium, vitamin C, and dietary fiber. Unfortunately, they are usually fried, which can add considerable fat to an otherwise virtually fat-free food. In this healthful side dish, we bake plantain slices in a coating of crushed blue corn chips. We use blue corn chips because they are so readily available—be sure to buy chips that are baked rather than fried, so as not to defeat the benefits of baking the plantain. You could easily substitute ¼ cup blue cornmeal, but then you wouldn't get to nibble your way through the rest of the chips as you cook.

For this dish you want to use a plantain that has ripened to the stage of turning yellow, which will be somewhat softer and sweeter than a green plantain would be. Let plantains ripen at room temperature; refrigeration stops the ripening process. We usually dollop a bit of reduced-fat sour cream on the coins and serve them with Mango Lime Salsa (page 259) on the side.

1 (about 10 ounces) yellow plantain

½ cup water

¼ cup plus 1 tablespoon fresh lime juice

1 ounce baked blue corn tortilla chips (about 18 chips), crushed (about ¼ cup)

2 tablespoons all-purpose flour

½ teaspoon ground cumin

Peel the plantain and slice it into ¼-inch rounds. Combine in a small bowl with the water and ¼ cup lime juice. Set aside for about 1 hour.

Place a heavy-gauge nonstick baking sheet in the oven and preheat the oven to 350F (175C). Mix the tortilla chip crumbs, flour, and cumin together in a large shallow bowl or a baking dish. Roll the plantain coins in the mixture to coat and let sit for 5 minutes.

Spray the preheated baking sheet with cooking spray. Arrange the plantain coins on the sheet in a single layer. Spray the coins with cooking spray and place the sheet on the bottom rack of the oven. Bake for 10 minutes. Spray the coins with cooking spray, turn them over, and bake for about 13 minutes more, until lightly browned. Drizzle with the remaining 1 tablespoon lime juice before serving.

GINGERED STIR-FRIED VEGETABLES

MAKES 6 SERVINGS

PER SERVING
Fat 0 g
Protein 2 g
Carbohydrates 7 g
Calories 40

This robust and flavorful side dish complements a range of entrées, and we use it constantly. Its two primary flavorings are ginger—which, as our friend Lizanne says, you can never have too much of—and oyster sauce, a pungent, salty concoction the Chinese use as a table condiment much as Americans do ketchup. Oyster sauce can be found in your supermarket's Asian section, along with all kinds of other goodies that are a boon to the healthy cook—sauces, flavorings, and condiments low in fat and potent in flavor. Look for oyster sauces thin enough to be pourable; they are considered of better quality than the thicker varieties.

Although we prefer to use the strong-tasting Chinese broccoli, or its equally distinguished Italian counterpart, broccoli rabe, this dish is assertive enough that regular broccoli will work just fine as well. Whichever veggies you use, Gingered Stir-Fried Vegetables are particularly good served with Lizanne's Gingered Drumsticks (page 92).

SAUCE

¼ cup oyster sauce

2 tablespoons dry sherry

1 tablespoon reduced-sodium soy sauce

½ teaspoon sugar

8 ounces Chinese broccoli or broccoli rabe, cut into 2-inch chunks

1 red bell pepper, cored, seeded, and cut into thin strips

1 small yellow onion, cut into ¼-inch wedges

¼ cup water

2 teaspoons grated fresh ginger

2 cloves garlic, minced

4 ounces shiitake mushrooms, cleaned, trimmed, and halved

Combine all ingredients for the sauce in a small bowl. Mix and set aside.

Preheat a nonstick stir-fry pan, a large nonstick skillet, or a wok over medium-high heat. Add the broccoli, bell pepper, onion, and water. Stir-fry until the broccoli turns bright green, about 2 minutes. Add the ginger and garlic, and stir-fry for about 1 minute. Add the mushrooms and stir-fry until all the liquid has been absorbed, about 20 seconds. Add the sauce and stir to coat and heat through, about 30 seconds more.

POLENTA-ENCRUSTED FRIED GREEN TOMATOES

MAKES 4 SERVINGS

PER SERVING
Fat 0.5 g
Protein 6 g
Carbohydrates 35 g
Calories 170

We were addicted to fried green tomatoes long before the movie with the café and the train and all lent them a certain retro cachet. They're basic, good, and plentiful in the fall, an abundance to which we always look forward eagerly. And if you grow your own tomatoes, you can have a steady supply through the summer as well. Just pick the tomatoes before they ripen and turn red.

In this recipe, a polenta crust baked onto the tomatoes approximates the crunch usually obtained by frying them in butter. Coarse Italian cornmeal gives a firmer, more defined crust than would the finer grain domestic cornmeal.

2 (about 1 pound total) green tomatoes

3 tablespoons all-purpose flour

1 cup polenta (coarse cornmeal)

2 large egg whites

2 tablespoons water

Preheat the oven to 500F (260C). Cut the tomatoes crosswise into ½-inch slices.

Scatter the flour over a plate. Put the cornmeal on a second plate. In a large, shallow bowl, lightly beat the egg whites with the water.

Dust the tomato slices with the flour, dip them in the egg white mixture, and turn to coat in the polenta. Spray a heavy-gauge nonstick baking sheet with cooking spray. Spray the tomato slices on both sides and lay them on the baking sheet. Bake for 10 minutes. Turn and bake for 8 to 10 minutes more, until the tomatoes are brown and firm to the touch.

Summer Vegetable Hash

You won't miss the fatty corned beef when you enjoy this satisfying vegetarian alternative for breakfast, lunch, or supper. Hash, of course, should be served with chili sauce, one of the great James Beard's most inspired pairings, according to food writer William Rice. Use a better-quality bottled chili sauce or make your own (page 172).

MAKES 4 SERVINGS

PER SERVING
Fat 0 g
Protein 6 g
Carbohydrates 28 g
Calories 130

8 to 10 small (about 1 pound total) white potatoes, quartered

⅓ cup water

1 red bell pepper, cored, seeded, and chopped

1 medium yellow onion, chopped

1 zucchini, chopped

1 yellow crookneck squash, chopped

2 teaspoons chopped fresh basil

⅔ cup evaporated skim milk

¼ teaspoon salt

¼ teaspoon ground white pepper

Put the potatoes and water in a microwave-safe container. Cover with plastic wrap and microwave on HIGH power until the potatoes are fork-tender, 2½ to 3 minutes.

Preheat a medium nonstick skillet over medium heat. Drain the potatoes and combine them in the pan with the bell pepper, onion, zucchini, yellow squash, basil, and evaporated milk. Stirring constantly, cook until all of the evaporated milk has been absorbed, 4 to 5 minutes. Stir in the salt and white pepper.

Variation

For a special treat, serve the hash topped with poached eggs, just as you would corned beef hash.

When the hash is just about done, add 2 tablespoons water to the skillet and break 4 eggs over the hash, 1 in each quarter of the pan. Cover and cook for 3 to 4 minutes more, until the eggs are set and cooked to the desired doneness. Cut the hash into four wedges, serving an egg in each portion.

Chili Sauce—Finishing Hash with a Flourish

MAKES ABOUT 1 CUP
(16 TABLESPOONS)

PER TABLESPOON
Fat 0 g
Protein 1 g
Carbohydrates 10 g
Calories 45

The late, great James Beard would definitely have approved of serving your hash with a homemade chili sauce. Here's one of our favorites.

1 green bell pepper, cored, seeded, and cut into chunks

1 yellow bell pepper, cored, seeded, and cut into chunks

1 yellow onion, cut into chunks

1 (14½-ounce) can diced tomatoes

1 (6-ounce) can tomato paste

⅓ cup packed dark brown sugar

¼ cup cider vinegar

2 teaspoons dry mustard

1 teaspoon ground allspice

¼ teaspoon ground cloves

¼ teaspoon ground cinnamon

¼ teaspoon ground ginger

¼ teaspoon ground nutmeg

¼ teaspoon celery seed

1 tablespoon cornstarch

1 tablespoon distilled white vinegar

Finely chop the bell peppers and onion in a food processor.

Transfer the peppers and onion to a large nonreactive saucepan. Add the tomatoes, tomato paste, brown sugar, cider vinegar, mustard, allspice, cloves, cinnamon, ginger, nutmeg, and celery seed. Bring to a boil and continue to boil rapidly, stirring occasionally, until thickened, about 20 minutes.

In a small bowl, dissolve the cornstarch in the white vinegar. Stir the mixture into the chili sauce just as it finishes cooking.

EGGPLANT PANINI

MAKES 6 SERVINGS

PER SERVING
Fat 2 g
Protein 11 g
Carbohydrates 21 g
Calories 150

These delightful little (well, actually not so little) Italian-style sandwiches, which are encased between layers of eggplant rather than bread, can serve equally well as plated appetizers or as brunch or luncheon fare. For a visually stunning first course, serve them in shallow bowls as you would ravioli, topped with warm Tomato Broth (page 266) and a few shavings of freshly grated Parmesan cheese.

There probably aren't enough water buffaloes in the world to supply all of the mozzarella cheese labeled "buffalo mozzarella." In fact, most sold outside Italy is made from cow's milk. But do look for delicate, flavorful fresh mozzarella in a cheese shop, better supermarket, or Italian grocery rather than using the dry, stringy, factory-made variety. An equal amount of chopped fresh basil can easily be substituted for the oregano.

2 medium (about 2 pounds total) eggplants

1 teaspoon coarse salt

1 large egg

2 egg whites

1 cup Italian-style breadcrumbs (prepared or page 23)

1 tablespoon garlic powder

4 ounces fresh mozzarella cheese, thinly sliced

2 tablespoons packed chopped fresh oregano

Trim and slice each eggplant crosswise into 6 (¼-inch) rounds. Sprinkle with the salt and set aside in a colander to drain for about 1 hour.

Pat the eggplant rounds dry with paper towels. In a large, shallow bowl, lightly beat the egg with the egg whites. Mix the breadcrumbs and garlic powder together on a plate.

Divide the cheese among 6 eggplant rounds and scatter 1 teaspoon of the oregano over each, leaving a slight border all around. Top each cheese-topped round with a second eggplant round. Carefully dip each panini into the egg mixture, using tongs or sliding a large, flat spatula underneath and pressing on top to keep the panini intact. Transfer the panini to the plate and sprinkle to coat with the breadcrumb mixture.

Preheat a large nonstick skillet over medium-high heat. Spray the top of each panini with cooking spray, carefully turn and place, sprayed side down, in the pan. Cook, turning once, until golden brown, 3 to 4 minutes per side.

JILL'S CRISPY ZUCCHINI ROUNDS

MAKES 4 SERVINGS

PER SERVING
Fat 0 g
Protein 2 g
Carbohydrates 3 g
Calories 20

We thank Jill Van Cleave, friend, colleague, and inexhaustible source of culinary information, for this quick, easy recipe. This was her response to a call one day when we were desperate for a simple alternative to the endless offering of stuffed, baked zucchini preparations. The salting softens the zucchini, which then cooks very fast, browning nicely in the process. Use the oregano or substitute an equal amount of whatever fresh herb best complements the entrée (or ½ teaspoon of the dried herb of your choice).

> 2 medium (about 12 ounces total) zucchini
>
> ½ tablespoon coarse salt
>
> 1 teaspoon chopped fresh oregano

Slice the zucchini into very thin rounds. Place the rounds in a colander, sprinkle with the coarse salt, and set aside for about 30 minutes.

Preheat a medium nonstick skillet over high heat. Blot the zucchini dry with paper towels. Spray the rounds lightly to coat with cooking spray and place in the pan. Stirring often, cook until the zucchini has browned, about 4 minutes. Toss with the oregano.

CREOLE OKRA

In addition to being tasty, okra is loaded with vitamin C, calcium, and iron. Look for pods that are firm, bright, unblemished, and smallish; smaller pods are tenderer than larger ones. Hot-oven baking not only cooks the okra without the addition of superfluous fat that frying would involve, but also dries and crisps it, doing away with the viscous coating often associated with boiled or steamed okra. We serve the okra with Creole Mustard Aïoli (page 254).

MAKES 4 SERVINGS

PER SERVING
Fat 2 g
Protein 7 g
Carbohydrates 24 g
Calories 140

¼ cup masa harina (see page 13)

½ tablespoon Creole seasoning (prepared or page 25)

½ cup yellow cornmeal

1 teaspoon onion powder

1 large egg

2 egg whites

8 ounces okra (about 24 pods), trimmed

Place a heavy-gauge nonstick baking sheet in the oven and preheat the oven to 500F (260C). Combine the masa harina and Creole seasoning in a plastic bag. In a second plastic bag, combine the cornmeal and onion powder. Lightly beat the egg with the egg whites in a large, shallow bowl.

Shake the okra, 4 or so at a time, in the masa harina mixture. Dip them in the egg mixture, then shake to coat in the cornmeal mixture. Spray the preheated baking sheet with cooking spray. Lay the okra on the baking sheet. Bake for 2 minutes. Spray the okra lightly with cooking spray, shake the pan, and bake for another 2 minutes. Spray any pods that look dry and bake about 2 minutes more, until golden brown all over.

CHIVE POTATO PANCAKES

MAKES 4 SERVINGS

PER SERVING
Fat 1.5 g
Protein 4 g
Carbohydrates 29 g
Calories 140

We came up with this crisp, flavorful pancake—a latke by another name—for Barry's mother, who just couldn't bear to eat Cousin Barbie's greasy latkes for one more Hanukkah. Barbie fries her potato pancakes in chicken fat. We bake ours, after soaking the potatoes in a water and vinegar mixture that firms them up, producing pancakes dotted with bits of intact potato rather than the typical nondescript mush. Serve our pancakes with Apple Chutney (page 265); serve Barbie's to somebody else.

2 (about 1¼ pounds total) baking potatoes

4 cups water

1 tablespoon vinegar

1 large egg

2 tablespoons potato starch

1 teaspoon salt

3 tablespoons snipped fresh chives

Ground black pepper to taste

Peel the potatoes and grate them with a large-hole grater. (You should have about 2½ cups of grated potatoes.) Combine with the water and vinegar in a medium bowl. Let soak for about 30 minutes.

Place a heavy-gauge nonstick baking sheet in the oven and preheat the oven to 450F (230C).

Strain the grated potatoes, squeeze out excess moisture, and blot dry with paper towels. In a medium bowl, lightly beat the egg and whisk in the potato starch to thoroughly blend. Whisk in the salt, chives, and pepper. Fold in the potatoes.

Spray the preheated baking sheet with cooking spray. Drop 8 pancakes onto the baking sheet, using about ¼ cup of the potato mixture for each. Flatten and lightly spray the pancakes with cooking spray. Bake for 7 minutes. Turn the pancakes over and bake about 7 minutes more, until golden brown.

GRAINS AND LEGUMES

MANY GRAINS AND legumes are so full of stuff that's good for you that we tend to forget the consequences of how we prepare them. When consumer advocates turned an analytical eye on Chinese take-out food a while ago, they blew the whistle on the gobs of hidden fat in innocent-looking dishes like fried rice. The same scrutiny would show the likes of falafel, *pad Thai*, rice cakes (the real ones fried on a griddle, not the cardboard cracker ones), and other fried grains as the dietary land mines they truly can be. And most of us now know instinctively that as good as beans are, and as good as they are for us nutritionally, the word "refried" undoubtedly bodes problems.

But fear not. We've restored fried rice to the realm of the righteous by stir-frying without oil, put beans back on the menu by "frying" in chicken broth, and returned hot-oven baked falafel to good health.

ELLIE'S FALAFEL

MAKES 4 SERVINGS

PER SERVING
Fat 1.5 g
Protein 6 g
Carbohydrates 20 g
Calories 120

This dish is for Barry's sister-in-law Eleanor, who loves Middle Eastern food. Ellie's been addicted to falafel ever since she first sampled it in Israel, where falafel-stuffed pitas (see page 181) are sold by vendors who stock an array of toppings from which customers choose. However, falafel, usually deep fried, has been a decided no-no since Ellie joined a women's health research project with very low fat dietary guidelines.

Although the croquettes, consisting principally of ground chickpeas, are often formed into balls, we make them as patties for easier baking and flipping. High in minerals and a decent source of protein, chickpeas, also called garbanzo beans, contain no saturated fat.

1½ cups cooked chickpeas

1 small yellow onion, peeled and cut into chunks

2 tablespoons fresh parsley leaves

1 tablespoon fresh lemon juice

1 teaspoon ground cumin

½ teaspoon ground coriander

½ teaspoon salt

4 tablespoons yellow cornmeal

In the bowl of a food processor, combine the chickpeas, onion, parsley, lemon juice, cumin, coriander, salt, and 2 tablespoons of the cornmeal. Process to a smooth puree. Transfer the puree to a bowl, cover, and refrigerate for about 15 minutes.

Preheat the oven to 450F (230C). Sprinkle the remaining 2 tablespoons cornmeal on a plate.

Form the chilled puree into 20 small patties, using 1 tablespoon of the mixture for each. Turn the cakes in the cornmeal to coat and place them on a heavy-gauge nonstick baking sheet. Bake for 6 minutes, flip the patties, and bake for about 6 minutes more, until they are just beginning to brown.

Serve 5 cakes per person, along with some of the sauce we make below, if desired.

Pitas with Your Patties

Instead of serving the falafel as an appetizer on a plate, you could serve it in a pita pocket with sauce and the toppings of your choice (such as diced tomato, pickles, and shredded lettuce), just like the ones sold at pita stands in Israel.

MAKES 4 SERVINGS

PER SERVING
(INCLUDING FALAFEL)
Fat 3.5 g
Protein 13 g
Carbohydrates 55 g
Calories 310

SAUCE

¼ cup diced zucchini

¼ cup reduced-fat sour cream

½ tablespoon snipped fresh dill

1 teaspoon fresh lemon juice

¼ teaspoon curry powder (prepared or page 26)

¼ teaspoon salt

4 pita pockets

20 cooked Ellie's Falafel patties (see opposite)

Combine all of the sauce ingredients in a bowl and mix together well. Snip open the tops of the pita pockets and fill each with 5 patties and 2 tablespoons of the sauce.

REFRIED BEANS

MAKES 4 SERVINGS

PER SERVING
Fat 0 g
Protein 12 g
Carbohydrates 36 g
Calories 190

Frijoles refritos **really translates as well-fried, not refried, but whatever you call it, the frying usually takes place in a lot of lard, typically producing a dish with around 15 grams of fat and at least 250 calories. We substitute broth in this spicy and eminently substantial variation, stripping the dish of fat and shaving off about a fourth of the calories.**

Our method cuts considerable time as well as fat. While it normally takes at least 20 minutes to prepare a typical refried bean recipe, these beans cook in about 10. By folding in some whole beans at the end, we achieve the chunky, coarse texture that is the hallmark of properly cooked refried beans, just as they serve them at Chicago's superb Frontera Grill. We like to serve each portion with a dollop of sour cream and a sprinkle of chopped cilantro.

1 large yellow onion, chopped (about 1 cup)

1½ cups defatted chicken broth (canned or page 19)

3 cups cooked pinto beans

1 medium tomato, chopped (about 1 cup)

½ tablespoon ground cumin

1 teaspoon ground coriander

1 teaspoon green hot sauce, or to taste

Preheat a medium nonstick skillet over medium-high heat. Add the onion. Stirring constantly, cook until it is just beginning to brown, 1 to 2 minutes. Add the broth and 2 cups of the beans. Reduce the heat to medium and cook, mashing the beans with the back of a spoon, 5 to 6 minutes. Stir in the tomato, cumin, coriander, hot sauce, and the remaining 1 cup beans. Cook and stir until the beans are very thick, 2 to 3 minutes.

BASMATI FRIED RICE WITH CURRIED CATFISH

This complex stir-fry is a complete meal by itself. The sauce is on the hot side, but not overwhelmingly so. It derives its kick from a Szechuan-style bean and garlic paste (labeled spicy garlic sauce) sold in Asian markets. Use a fairly mild curry powder, which will complement the spiciness of the sauce and the nuttiness of the rice better than a more aggressive curry would.

MAKES 6 SERVINGS

PER SERVING
Fat 4.5 g
Protein 17 g
Carbohydrates 41 g
Calories 260

4 cups cooked basmati rice

½ cup spicy garlic sauce

2 tablespoons reduced-sodium soy sauce

2 tablespoons curry powder (prepared or page 26)

1 medium yellow onion, chopped (about 1 cup)

¼ cup water

1 pound catfish fillets, roughly chopped (about 2 cups)

Combine the rice, garlic sauce, soy sauce, and curry powder in a medium bowl. Mix and set aside.

Preheat a nonstick stir-fry pan, a large nonstick skillet, or a wok over high heat. Add the onion and water, and cook, stirring, until the water evaporates and the onion begins to color, about 1 minute. Add the catfish and cook, stirring, for 1 minute. Add the rice mixture and stir-fry until all the liquid has been absorbed, about 1 minute more.

Cook's Tip: To cook basmati rice, combine 1 cup rice and 2 cups water in a small saucepan. Bring to a boil. Cover and reduce the heat to low. Simmer for 20 minutes, then remove from the heat and set aside, covered, for 5 minutes. If you substitute brown rice, which would also work nicely in this recipe, follow package directions for cooking.

GRIDDLED RISOTTO CAKES

MAKES 6 SERVINGS

PER SERVING
Fat 0.5 g
Protein 6 g
Carbohydrates 38 g
Calories 190

We include the full, start-to-finish recipe for our favorite citrus risotto below, but you can, of course, mold and griddle risotto cakes using 3 cups of any leftover risotto. The cakes make a nice accompaniment to a variety of meats and poultry. Try them with Crispy Lemon Quail (page 82), especially if the cakes are made with the citrus risotto.

3¾ cups defatted chicken broth (canned or page 19)

1¼ cups Arborio rice

1 tablespoon grated lemon zest

¼ cup fresh lemon juice

1 tablespoon chopped fresh parsley

2 tablespoons grated Parmesan cheese

In a medium saucepan, bring the broth to a boil over high heat. Reduce the heat to the lowest possible setting and maintain at a simmer.

Preheat a large, heavy pan over high heat. Reduce the heat to medium and add the rice. Cook, stirring constantly, until the rice is lightly toasted, 1 to 2 minutes. Stirring vigorously, slowly add 1 cup of the broth. When most of the broth has been absorbed, stir in another ½ cup. Continue to cook and stir, adding the rest of the broth in ½ cup increments. With the last addition of broth, stir in the lemon zest, lemon juice, parsley, and Parmesan cheese. Cook, stirring, until all the liquid has been absorbed and the rice is creamy.

Spray an 8-inch round cake pan with cooking spray and scrape the risotto into the pan. Cover and refrigerate for at least 3 hours to firm.

Run a knife around the edge of the pan to loosen the risotto cake, turn the pan upside down, and bang it on a cutting board to release the cake. Cut the risotto cake into 6 wedges and spray each with cooking spray.

Preheat a nonstick griddle or a large nonstick skillet over high heat. Place the risotto wedges on the hot griddle, sprayed side down. Reduce the heat to medium-high and cook until crisp and well browned, about 3 minutes. Spray again with cooking spray, turn the wedges over, and cook until well browned on the other side, about 3 minutes more. Turn each wedge over again onto the serving plate, so that the side with the more granular surface is exposed.

Variation: Risotto Pronto

Our favorite way to prepare wonderful, creamy risotto—in a fraction of the time it takes on the stovetop and without all the stirring—is in a pressure cooker. Unlike your mother's, the new models of pressure cookers are safe, sleek, and the best way to whip up no-fail stocks and stews in minutes.

To make the recipe above in a pressure cooker, preheat the cooker over high heat. Without reducing the heat, as you would in a saucepan, add the 1¼ cups rice and stir until lightly toasted, 1 to 2 minutes. Stir in the broth all at once (use only 2½ cups) along with the ¼ cup lemon juice. Bring to full pressure and reduce the heat to stabilize pressure. Cook for 7 minutes. Quick-release according to manufacturer's directions and stir in the lemon zest, parsley, and cheese as called for in the original recipe.

VEGETABLE FRIED RICE

MAKES 4 SERVINGS

PER SERVING
Fat 1.5 g
Protein 5 g
Carbohydrates 27 g
Calories 150

We keep white rice on hand in the freezer (the extra stuff from Chinese take-out) to make Vegetable Fried Rice. If the rice is cold, it is easier to separate the grains as you put it into the pan, and cold white rice also tends to cook better. This basic, versatile dish is so low in fat—only 1.5 grams—because we stir-fry in water instead of peanut oil, finishing everything off with a flourish of soy sauce and sherry.

2 tablespoons reduced-sodium soy sauce

1 tablespoon dry sherry

1 medium zucchini, chopped

1 medium red bell pepper, cored, seeded, and chopped

2 green onions, trimmed to white and light green parts and chopped (about ¼ cup)

2 tablespoons water

1 large egg

2 cups cooked white rice, chilled

Mix the soy sauce and sherry together in a small bowl and set aside.

Preheat a nonstick stir-fry pan, a large nonstick skillet, or a wok over high heat. Add the zucchini, bell pepper, green onions, and water. Stir-fry 30 seconds. Add the egg and cook about 1 minute more, stirring the vegetables with the egg as it scrambles. Add the rice and stir-fry 2 minutes more. Add the sauce mixture and toss to coat.

CRUNCHY BLACK BEAN CAKES WITH SALSA

This appetizer is somewhat evocative of a good black bean soup in solid form. Serve it with a bit of Corn and Orange Tomato Salsa (page 261), a dollop of sour cream, and a sprinkle of cilantro. The main ingredient, of course, is mineral-rich, fat-free, low-sodium black beans. Use either dried turtle beans that have been cooked or canned beans that have been rinsed and drained.

MAKES 4 SERVINGS

PER SERVING
Fat 0.5
Protein 5 g
Carbohydrates 20 g
Calories 90

2 tablespoons yellow cornmeal

1½ cups cooked black beans

½ cup chopped yellow onion

1 small tomato, seeded and diced

2 tablespoons finely chopped fresh cilantro

1 clove garlic, minced

1 tablespoon reduced-fat sour cream

1 teaspoon ground cumin

½ teaspoon salt

Pinch of cayenne pepper

Corn and Orange Tomato Salsa

Scatter the cornmeal on a plate.

In a large bowl, mash the beans until crumbly, leaving a few intact. Mix in the onion, tomato, cilantro, garlic, and sour cream. Add the cumin, salt, and cayenne and mix well.

Form 8 cakes, using about ¼ cup of the mixture for each. Turn the cakes in the cornmeal to coat. Place them on a large plate. Cover and refrigerate for at least 30 minutes to firm.

Preheat the oven to 500F (260C).

Spray a heavy-gauge nonstick baking sheet with cooking spray. Place the bean cakes on the sheet and bake for 10 minutes. Turn over and bake for about 10 minutes more, until browned and crisp. Serve 2 cakes per person with salsa.

PITA POCKET CHIPS

MAKES 8 SERVINGS

PER SERVING
Fat 0
Protein 2 g
Carbohydrates 13 g
Calories 60

Pita bread is made with either white or whole-wheat flour. For this appetizer, in which the pita is cut up in typical Middle Eastern fashion rather than stuffed, we prefer the variety made with white flour. Serve with Cumin Mayonnaise (page 253), Mixed Pepper Salsa (page 260), Apple Chutney (page 265) or creamy hummus (see opposite).

½ teaspoon salt

⅛ teaspoon ground cumin

3 pita pockets

Preheat the oven to 375F (190C). Mix together the salt and cumin in a small bowl.

Slit each pita pocket open into 2 circles. Cut each pita circle into 8 wedges. Arrange the wedges in a single layer on a heavy-gauge nonstick baking sheet. Spray lightly with cooking spray. Scatter the cumin-salt mixture over the wedges and bake until very crisp, 7 to 8 minutes. Serve 6 wedges per person.

Roasted Red Pepper Hummus

The perfect accompaniment for pita chips, this simple recipe can be whipped up in even less time than the chips.

MAKES 8 SERVINGS

PER SERVING
Fat 3 g
Protein 5 g
Carbohydrates 12 g
Calories 90

1½ cups cooked chickpeas

6 ounces roasted red bell peppers, drained

1 cup reduced-fat sour cream

⅓ cup fresh lemon juice

⅓ cup chopped fresh cilantro

½ teaspoon ground cumin

2 cloves garlic, peeled and chopped

Combine all ingredients in the bowl of a food processor or blender and puree until smooth.

TOFU *PAD THAI*

MAKE 4 SERVINGS

PER SERVING
Fat 4.5 g
Protein 15 g
Carbohydrates 71 g
Calories 380

Our adaptation of the classic Thai street food, *pad Thai*, can serve as an entrée for four, a side dish for six, or an appetizer for eight. It features tofu, which has advanced beyond its somewhat hippie reputation of a few years ago now that we are all more concerned with healthful eating. A soybean curd product, tofu is a meatless source of high-quality protein that's relatively low in calories and has almost no saturated fat. There is even a new light tofu that has only a fraction of the total fat.

Rice stick noodles, which have virtually no fat, are now available in many supermarkets; look for noodles about ¼-inch wide. Chinese or Japanese rice vinegar is also stocked in supermarkets, although we buy ours in Asian groceries, where it is usually quite a bit cheaper. Serve the *pad Thai* with lime wedges on the side.

8 ounces rice stick noodles

4 cups warm water

¼ cup plus 2 tablespoons rice vinegar

¼ cup plus 2 tablespoons sugar

¼ cup fish sauce

¼ teaspoon hot sauce

3 green onions, trimmed to white and light green parts and sliced on the diagonal

8 ounces (about 2 cups) mung bean sprouts

5 ounces (about ⅔ cup) extra-firm light tofu, cubed

1 large egg, beaten

¼ cup chopped fresh cilantro

¼ cup crushed unsalted dry-roasted peanuts

Combine the rice stick noodles and water in a large bowl. Set aside until the noodles are soft, about 30 minutes. Drain.

In a small bowl, mix together the vinegar, sugar, fish sauce, and hot sauce.

Preheat a nonstick stir-fry pan, a large nonstick skillet, or a wok over medium heat. Add the noodles and the vinegar mixture. Stirring constantly, cook until all the liquid has been absorbed, about 3 minutes. Add the green onions, sprouts, and tofu. Stir-fry about 1 minute. Push the contents of the pan to one side. On the other side of the pan, lightly scramble the egg, and then mix the scrambled egg in with the other ingredients.

Garnish with the cilantro and peanuts.

POLENTA PANINI

MAKES 4 SERVINGS

PER SERVING
Fat 5 g
Protein 10 g
Carbohydrates 32 g
Calories 220

As a plated appetizer, we serve these little cornmeal cake sandwiches in shallow bowls, generously drizzled with Tomato Broth (page 266). They also make interesting cocktail party finger food. Use a 6-inch premade polenta log (they're readily available, both plain and flavored, in supermarkets), or make your own polenta from scratch (see opposite).

1½ cups Italian-style breadcrumbs (prepared or page 231)

1 large egg

2 egg whites

12 very thin slices fontina cheese

12 ounces polenta, cut into 24 (¼-inch) rounds

¼ cup shredded fresh basil

Heap the breadcrumbs on a plate. In a large, shallow bowl, beat the egg and egg whites together lightly.

Place 1 slice of cheese on each of 12 of the polenta rounds. Sprinkle each with 1 teaspoon of the basil and top with a second polenta round. Taking care to hold the "sandwiches" together with tongs or fingers, dip each into the egg mixture, then turn in the breadcrumbs to coat. Set the panini aside for about 5 minutes.

Preheat a nonstick griddle or a large nonstick skillet over high heat.

Spray 1 side of each panini with cooking spray and place them, sprayed side down, on the griddle. (If you use a skillet rather than a griddle, you may need to cook the panini in batches.)

Cook for 2 minutes. Spray the cakes again, turn them over, and reduce the heat to medium. Cover and cook until the panini are very brown, about 2 minutes more. Serve 3 panini per person.

Polenta from Scratch

Quick, easy, and really better than store-bought, homemade polenta can be made with buttermilk; if you're in the mood for a real splurge, substitute melted butter for the buttermilk. If you can readily find coarse Italian cornmeal, use it instead of the finer variety.

MAKES 12 OUNCES;
4 SERVINGS

PER SERVING
Fat 0 g
Protein 2 g
Carbohydrates 14 g
Calories 70

1⅓ cups water

¼ cup buttermilk

⅛ teaspoon salt

½ cup yellow or white cornmeal

In a small saucepan, combine the water, buttermilk, and salt over medium heat. Slowly whisk in the cornmeal. Reduce the heat to low. Stirring constantly, cook until the mixture is thick, smooth, and easily separates from the sides of the pan, 5 to 10 minutes. Spray a 6-inch mini loaf pan to coat lightly with cooking spray. Pour the polenta into the pan, cover, and refrigerate for at least 1 hour before slicing.

WILD RICE CAKES WITH SMOKED TROUT

MAKES 4 SERVINGS

PER SERVING
Fat 2.5 g
Protein 12 g
Carbohydrates 23 g
Calories 160

COOKING WILD RICE

To cook wild rice (which should always be rinsed first), combine ½ cup rice and 1½ cups water in a small saucepan. Bring to a boil, cover, reduce the heat to low, and cook for 40 minutes. Set aside off the heat for 15 minutes before uncovering.

Wild rice, which is really long-grain marsh grass, is native to Minnesota and Wisconsin, and is also commercially cultivated. It has a slightly chewy consistency and a distinctively nutty flavor that contrasts nicely with the smokiness of the fish. Use smoked trout or whitefish, either of which is available at many supermarket fish counters, or slightly more exotic smoked sable or sturgeon. We usually serve two cakes as an entrée, a single cake as an appetizer.

2 cups cooked wild rice

4 ounces (about ⅔ cup) smoked trout, skinned and flaked

2 green onions, trimmed to white and light green parts and diced

¼ cup chopped fresh parsley

1 tablespoon reduced-fat sour cream

¼ cup Italian-style breadcrumbs (prepared or page 23)

2 teaspoons snipped fresh chives

½ teaspoon salt

⅛ teaspoon ground white pepper

Combine the rice, trout, green onions, parsley, and sour cream in a large bowl. Add the breadcrumbs, chives, salt, and pepper. Mix thoroughly.

Form 8 cakes, using about ⅓ cup of the mixture for each. Place the cakes on a large plate, flattening each into a 3-inch disk. Cover and refrigerate for about 20 minutes, until firm to the touch.

Meanwhile, put a heavy-gauge nonstick baking sheet in the oven and preheat the oven to 450F (230C).

Spray the preheated baking sheet with cooking spray. Place the rice cakes on the sheet and bake for 5 minutes. Spray the cakes, turn them over, and bake for about 5 minutes more, until well browned. Serve 2 cakes per person.

WILD RICE PANCAKES

MAKES 6 SERVINGS

PER SERVING
Fat 3.5 g
Protein 7 g
Carbohydrates 28 g
Calories 170

These savory pancakes go well with many sauced entrées. We particularly like them with Stir-Fried Asian Frogs' Legs (page 148). They are heavenly topped with salmon caviar or with one of the flavored caviars, but also good with lumpfish caviar from the supermarket or just sour cream and no caviar. You can also heap them on a platter for a buffet, served with a selection of toppings—sour cream, Apple Chutney (page 265), Caper Cream (page 263), and perhaps some slivers of smoked salmon. See page 194 for directions on cooking wild rice.

2 cups cooked wild rice

1 cup all-purpose buttermilk baking mix

½ teaspoon salt

¼ teaspoon ground white pepper

1 large egg

⅔ cup skim milk

Scant ½ cup reduced-fat sour cream

1 tablespoon plus 2 teaspoons caviar (optional)

Snipped chives, for garnish

Place a heavy-gauge nonstick baking sheet in the oven and preheat the oven to 450F (230C).

Mix the rice, baking mix, salt, and white pepper together in a large bowl. In a small bowl, whisk the egg with the milk. Stir the mixture into the rice to combine.

Spray the preheated baking sheet with cooking spray. Drop 18 pancakes onto the sheet, using a generous 2 tablespoons of the rice mixture for each. Flatten pancakes into 2½- to 3-inch disks. Place the baking sheet on the middle rack of the oven and bake for 5 minutes.

Spray the pancakes with cooking spray and turn them over. Move the baking sheet to the bottom rack of the oven and bake for about 5 minutes more, until well browned.

Top each pancake with a generous 1 teaspoon of sour cream and ¼ teaspoon of caviar, if desired. Garnish with a sprinkling of chives. Serve 3 pancakes per person.

CHILI LIME TORTILLA CHIPS

MAKE 6 SERVINGS

PER SERVING
Fat 1 g
Protein 2 g
Carbohydrates 17 g
Calories 80

The chili lime chips turning up on supermarket shelves are inviting, but all too many brands are high in fat. This is our alternative, preferably made with yellow corn tortillas, which seem to crisp faster than those made with white cornmeal. Heap them on a platter with little bowls of different salsas on the side.

8 (6-inch) corn tortillas

¼ cup fresh lime juice

1 teaspoon chili powder

Preheat the oven to 425F (220C).

Cut each tortilla into 6 wedges. Paint each wedge on both sides with lime juice and sprinkle with chili powder, spreading the seasoning over the wedge with your fingers. Place the wedges on a heavy-gauge nonstick baking sheet. Bake for about 4 minutes. Turn over and bake 4 minutes more, until toasted.

EGGS

IF BREAKFAST IS the most important meal of the day, it sure seems hard to get the day off to a good start sometimes. Even setting the cholesterol factor aside for a moment, many of the old standbys are awash in fat grams from the yolks, the sausage, or the butter on the griddle, in the batter, or atop the pancake or French toast. And since breakfast is one of those comfort meals some folks eat at noon or at night, the quandary hardly dissipates with the passage of the day.

In the recipes that follow, we've pared superfluous fat from the preparation of many breakfast favorites. We also revamped such other egg-based dishes as crepes, blintzes, and Monte Cristos, allowing you to decide for yourself how to allot these fat grams—when to splurge on whole eggs with yolks, when to add a pat or two of butter to finish a dish.

WESTERN OMELET SANDWICH

MAKES 2 SERVINGS

PER SERVING
Fat 7 g
Protein 19 g
Carbohydrates 25 g
Calories 230

This was Barry's all-time favorite midmorning sustenance during his Los Angeles years, bought every morning from a hole-in-the-wall sandwich shack incongruously nestled amid the office towers of Sunset Boulevard.

Our oven-baked rendition not only cuts the fat but also makes omelet making easy even for those who, like Kevin, can't be relied upon to flip a perfect omelet every time up at the skillet. It's really more like a big friendly mess of scrambled eggs folded up like an omelet at the last minute. The recipe is easily doubled to serve 4.

¼ cup chopped red bell pepper

2 tablespoons chopped green onion (about 1 green onion, trimmed to white and light green parts)

1 large egg

2 egg whites

1 tablespoon skim milk

¼ cup chopped cooked ham

⅛ teaspoon salt

Pinch of cayenne pepper

2 tablespoons grated Swiss cheese

4 slices light oatmeal bread, toasted

2 tablespoons ketchup

Preheat the oven to 350F (175C).

Spray an 8-inch round glass pie plate or casserole lightly with cooking spray. Scatter the bell pepper and green onion in the dish. Spray the vegetables lightly and bake for about 10 minutes, until the onion is translucent and the bell pepper has softened.

Combine the egg, egg whites, milk, ham, salt, and cayenne in a small bowl. Mix to blend. Pour the egg mixture over the baked onion and bell pepper. Bake for about 5 minutes, until the egg mixture is softly set. Remove from the oven, stir to disperse the vegetables through the egg mixture, and scatter the cheese on top. Fold half of the omelet over to enclose the cheese, then cut it in half.

On each of 2 slices of toast, spread 1 tablespoon ketchup. Place half of the omelet on each and top with a second slice of toast. Cut each sandwich in half.

BREAKFAST BURRITO

MAKES 8 SERVINGS

PER SERVING
Fat 8.5 g
Protein 28 g
Carbohydrates 45 g
Calories 440

Served up with mango or avocado slices and dark, rich coffee, breakfast burritos are great for casual brunches. Flour tortillas used to be a big no-no for healthy diners, but there is now a tasty variety available in the supermarket refrigerator case that has almost no fat. The Chihuahua cheese can be replaced with shredded mozzarella or Monterey Jack or any other mild white cheese.

Those predisposed to fast food burritos on the go may want to consider making their own. Even using whole eggs, our burrito weighs in at only 8.5 grams of fat—Taco Bell's racks up 24 grams of fat.

8 large eggs

2 tablespoons skim milk

½ teaspoon salt

¼ teaspoon ground black pepper

8 large nonfat flour tortillas

½ cup grated *asadero* (Chihuahua) cheese

2 cups cooked Chorizo (page 51)

2 cups Mixed Pepper Salsa (page 260)

½ cup reduced-fat sour cream (optional)

Preheat the oven to 350F (175C).

Spray a 2-quart glass casserole with cooking spray. Crack the eggs into the casserole and beat lightly. Beat in the milk, salt, and pepper. Bake for 10 minutes. Wrap the tortillas in foil and place them in the oven. Remove the casserole from the oven, stir the contents with a fork to break the eggs up, and add the cheese. Return the casserole to the oven and bake for about 5 minutes more, until the mixture is cooked through and puffed up. Remove the casserole from the oven and stir again with a fork. Remove and unwrap the tortillas.

In the center of each tortilla, put ¼ cup of the chorizo, ¼ cup of the eggs, ¼ cup of the salsa, and 1 tablespoon sour cream, if desired. Fold 2 opposite sides of the tortilla in over the filling, then fold in the side closest to you and roll up the burrito toward the far side.

Variation

To pare even more fat from the burrito, use your favorite reduced-fat white cheese and 2 cups nonfat liquid egg substitute instead of the eggs, or substitute 8 egg whites for 4 of the whole eggs.

HAM AND CHEESE FRITTATA

MAKES 4 SERVINGS

PER SERVING
Fat 5 g
Protein 12 g
Carbohydrates 3 g
Calories 110

A frittata is a large, Italian omelet in which the filling ingredients are premixed rather than folded in separately. In Spain, they make a similar egg dish, called a tortilla, which is a favorite tapas item. Since it can be served at room temperature, the dish is perfect for the buffet, no matter what you call it. While baking in a skillet, the bottom of the frittata gets very brown, presenting an attractively crusty top when it is flipped over onto a serving plate.

2 large eggs

2 egg whites

⅓ cup skim milk

2 tablespoons shredded Parmesan cheese

1 tablespoon thinly sliced fresh basil leaves

½ teaspoon salt

⅛ teaspoon ground white pepper

¾ cup chopped cooked ham

1 small tomato, peeled, seeded, and chopped (about ⅔ cup)

Place a medium cast-iron skillet or a nonstick skillet with an oven-safe handle in the oven and preheat the oven to 350F (175C).

In a medium bowl, whisk together the eggs, egg whites, and milk. Mix in the Parmesan cheese, basil, salt, and pepper, then the ham and the tomato.

If using a cast-iron skillet, spray the preheated skillet with cooking spray. Pour the egg mixture into the skillet and bake until the edges of the frittata have set and it is lightly browned, 20 to 25 minutes.

Remove the frittata from the oven and allow it to cool for at least 10 minutes before slicing.

Variations: A Frittata for All Tastes

Following the directions above, a few ingredient changes will produce a plethora of frittata variations, surely a selection to suit any mood.

Vidalia Onion and Mixed Pepper Frittata

For the ham and tomato in the original recipe above, substitute:

1 small Vidalia onion, sliced (about 1 cup)

1 green bell pepper, cored, seeded, and sliced (about 1 cup)

1 red bell pepper, cored, seeded, and sliced (about 1 cup)

Potato and Spinach Frittata

For the ham and tomato in the original recipe above, substitute:

1 medium red potato, peeled and shredded (about 1 cup)

1 small yellow onion, sliced (about ½ cup)

1 (10-ounce) package chopped frozen spinach, thawed and squeezed dry

Artichoke and Roasted Pepper Frittata

For the ham and tomato in the original recipe above, substitute:

6 ounces roasted red bell pepper, drained and sliced (about ½ cup)

2 green onions, trimmed to the white and light green parts, chopped (about ¼ cup)

1 (9-ounce) package frozen artichoke hearts, thawed

GRILLED CHICKEN MONTE CRISTOS

MAKES 4 SERVINGS

PER SERVING
Fat 4.5 g
Protein 18 g
Carbohydrates 23 g
Calories 210

Cooking Monte Cristo sandwiches on the stovetop, as anyone who's attempted to make them at home knows, can be time consuming and cumbersome, since each individual sandwich needs to be covered in order for the cheese to melt properly. By baking them in the oven, we not only save the fat of frying, but speed up the process as well. Now you can enjoy this cross between French toast and a grilled cheese sandwich with little mess and less worry over fat. If you don't have challah or another egg bread on hand, substitute a firm-textured white bread.

Serve the Monte Cristos with a soup or salad for lunch or brunch.

1 plum tomato

8 fresh basil leaves

8 slices challah or other egg bread

8 slices grilled chicken breast (about 6 ounces total)

4 thin slices smoked mozzarella cheese

Ground black pepper, to taste

1 large egg

2 egg whites

¼ cup skim milk

1 teaspoon paprika

½ teaspoon garlic powder

Place a heavy-gauge nonstick baking sheet in the oven and preheat the oven to 400F (205C).

Trim and cut the tomato into 8 rounds. Roll up the basil leaves and then slice them on the diagonal into thin strips.

Place 4 slices of the bread in an 11 × 7-inch baking dish. On each bread slice, layer 1 slice chicken, 1 slice mozzarella, 2 tomato rounds side by side, ½ tablespoon of the basil strips, pepper as desired, and a second slice of chicken. Top each with a second slice of bread.

In a small bowl, beat together the egg, egg whites, milk, paprika, and garlic powder. Pour the egg mixture over the sandwiches and let stand about 10 minutes for the egg mixture to be absorbed.

Spray the preheated baking sheet with cooking spray. Transfer the sandwiches to the sheet with a spatula and bake for 8 minutes. Turn and cook for about 8 minutes more, until well browned and firm to the touch.

VEGETABLE MONTE CRISTOS

MAKES 4 SERVINGS

PER SERVING
Fat 8 g
Protein 13 g
Carbohydrates 21 g
Calories 200

Perfect for a light, meatless meal, these Monte Cristos are made by layering vegetables and goat cheese between slices of Italian or rye bread. The yellow summer squash, which some call yellow zucchini, should not be confused with winter crookneck squash. The 3½-ounce blocks of goat cheese now sold in many supermarkets are perfect for this recipe; simply quarter the block lengthwise. Creamy Montrachet is a nice choice.

1 (10-ounce) package fresh spinach

1 small, thin yellow summer squash (3 to 4 ounces)

1 (3½-ounce) package fresh goat cheese with chives

8 slices Italian bread or oval rye bread

⅓ cup thinly sliced red onion

1 large egg

2 egg whites

¼ cup skim milk

Place a heavy-gauge nonstick baking sheet in the oven and preheat the oven to 400F (205C).

Stem the spinach and blanch by immersing it very briefly in boiling water. Drain immediately, refresh briefly in a bowl of ice water, and squeeze dry in paper towels.

Trim the squash and quarter it lengthwise. Cut the cheese into 4 long pieces.

Place 4 slices of the bread in an 11 × 7-inch baking dish. On each, layer 1 slice squash, 2 tablespoons spinach, 1 piece of goat cheese, and a scattering of onion. Top with a second slice of bread.

In a small bowl, beat together the egg, egg whites, and milk. Pour the egg mixture over the sandwiches and let stand about 10 minutes for the egg mixture to be absorbed.

Spray the preheated baking sheet lightly with cooking spray. Transfer the sandwiches to the sheet with a spatula and bake for 8 minutes. Turn and bake for about 8 minutes more, until well browned and firm to the touch.

BANANA FRENCH TOAST

MAKES 4 SERVINGS

PER SERVING
Fat 6 g
Protein 8 g
Carbohydrates 41 g
Calories 270

This rich, custardy stuffed French toast is reminiscent of bananas Foster, with the indulgent addition of some chopped pecans, permissible only because we've saved so many fat grams by not cooking the toast in butter. It's also very versatile—serve warm with syrup for breakfast, with frozen yogurt for Sunday brunch, or even with ice cream and Strawberry Sauce (page 217) for a special-occasion dessert. The slices of bread should be about ½-inch thick.

8 slices challah or other egg bread

2 bananas, halved lengthwise and then halved again crosswise

2 tablespoons chopped pecans

1 large egg

2 egg whites

¼ cup buttermilk

2 tablespoons golden rum

2 tablespoons packed dark brown sugar

1 teaspoon confectioners' sugar

Place a heavy-gauge nonstick baking sheet in the oven and preheat the oven to 400F (205C).

Lay 4 slices of the bread in an 11 × 7-inch baking dish. On each slice, lay 2 banana slices, scatter ½ tablespoon pecans, and top with a second slice of bread.

In a small bowl, beat together the egg, egg whites, buttermilk, rum, and brown sugar. Pour the egg mixture over the sandwiches. Turn the sandwiches over so that the mixture will be evenly absorbed, and let sit for about 10 minutes, then press the edges down to seal.

Spray the preheated baking sheet with cooking spray. Using a spatula, transfer the sandwiches to the baking sheet and bake for 10 minutes. Turn over and bake for 6 to 7 minutes more, until well browned and bubbly. Dust each portion with about ¼ teaspoon confectioners' sugar.

STRAWBERRY FRENCH TOAST

MAKES 4 SERVINGS

PER SERVING
Fat 2 g
Protein 9 g
Carbohydrates 30 g
Calories 180

Delectable any way you serve it, this French toast is equally good as traditional breakfast fare with maple syrup or Strawberry Sauce (page 217), or sliced on the diagonal into individual dessert sandwiches and garnished with frozen yogurt.

8 slices oatmeal bread

8 strawberries, hulled and sliced

¼ cup skim milk

1 large egg

2 egg whites

1 tablespoon Grand Marnier liqueur

½ tablespoon pure vanilla extract

2 tablespoons packed dark brown sugar

½ teaspoon ground allspice

Lay 4 slices of the bread in an 11 × 7-inch baking dish. Scatter strawberry slices over each. Top each with a second slice of bread.

In a small bowl, beat together the milk, egg, egg whites, liqueur, vanilla, brown sugar, and allspice. Pour the egg mixture over the sandwiches and let stand about 5 minutes for the egg mixture to be absorbed.

Preheat a nonstick griddle or large nonstick skillet over medium-high heat. Spray the griddle with cooking spray. Transfer the sandwiches to the griddle, using a spatula. Cook for 3 minutes, pressing the layers together lightly with a large spatula. Spray each portion and turn it over. Cook until firm and golden, about 3 minutes more.

CINNAMON FRENCH TOAST

Cut your own inch-thick slices of bread for this classic dish; challah, which makes the absolutely best ever French toast, is usually available unsliced. It's equally good drizzled with maple syrup or dolloped with strawberry jam. The 6 eggs for four servings is an admitted indulgence; use 1½ cups nonfat liquid egg substitute if you prefer, or substitute 4 egg whites for 2 of the eggs. However, if you do use the whole eggs and have the time, let the battered bread sit overnight in the refrigerator—the more egg absorbed, the richer and more custardy the toast will be. Freshly grated nutmeg adds a nice touch.

8 very thick slices challah or other egg bread

6 large eggs

½ cup skim milk

1 tablespoon sugar

1 teaspoon ground cinnamon

½ teaspoon grated nutmeg

Lay the bread in a single layer in a 13 × 9-inch baking dish.

In a medium bowl, lightly beat the eggs. Whisk in the milk, sugar, cinnamon, and nutmeg. Pour the mixture over the bread and turn to coat. Let stand about 30 minutes for the bread to absorb the coating, occasionally spooning the batter over the slices.

Preheat a nonstick griddle or large nonstick skillet over medium-high heat. Transfer the toast to the griddle, using a spatula, and cook for 2 minutes. Turn the toast over, reduce the heat to medium-low, and cook until the toast is well browned and springs back to the touch, about 3 minutes more.

MAKES 4 SERVINGS

PER SERVING
Fat 11 g
Protein 16 g
Carbohydrates 35 g
Calories 310

ORANGE CREPES

MAKES 6 SERVINGS

PER SERVING
Fat 3 g
Protein 4 g
Carbohydrates 17 g
Calories 110

Think of this as sort of a dressed-down crepes Suzette, with neither the fat and calories nor the pretensions usually associated with the classic French pancakes. With a good-quality nonstick pan, you can cook the crepes with no greasing at all, and they'll still pop out with no problem—you hardly need a special crepe pan. We finish the crepes with a drizzle of orange juice and a dusting of confectioners' sugar. For a slightly grander touch, see the Variation (opposite).

Classically prepared crepes have about 9 grams of fat and 190 calories per serving, compared with our 3 grams of fat and 110 calories. Crepes Suzette normally run about 16 grams of fat and 360 calories, while our Suzette-like flourish brings the calorie total up to about 190 without adding more fat.

1 tablespoon unsalted butter, melted

1 large egg

1 egg white

⅔ cup skim milk

¼ teaspoon salt

⅔ cup all-purpose flour

2 tablespoons granulated sugar

2 tablespoons orange juice

confectioners' sugar for dusting

Combine the butter, egg, egg white, milk, and salt in a medium bowl. Add the flour and whisk until smooth. Set aside about 10 minutes to thicken.

Preheat a small nonstick skillet over medium heat. To make each crepe, put about 3 tablespoons of the batter into the pan, swirling the pan to coat the surface evenly. Cook until the edges are firm and the crepe is very lightly browned, about 1 minute.

Sprinkle ½ teaspoon granulated sugar over each crepe and drizzle with ½ teaspoon orange juice. Serve 2 crepes per person, rolled up and dusted with confectioners' sugar.

Variation: Almost Crepes Suzette

To finish your crepes with a bit more traditional flourish, combine ½ cup orange marmalade or apricot preserves and 2 tablespoons orange liqueur, brandy, or orange juice in a small saucepan over medium heat. Cook until the marmalade or preserves have melted, about 3 minutes. Spoon a generous 2 tablespoons over each serving.

MAKES 6 SERVINGS

PER SERVING (INCLUDING CREPES)
Fat 3 g
Protein 4 g
Carbohydrates 17 g
Calories 190

CHEESE BLINTZES

MAKES 12 BLINTZES

PER BLINTZ
Fat 4.5 g
Protein 8 g
Carbohydrates 11 g
Calories 105

It's hard to get a really good blintz outside of New York—maybe it's something in the air. But if you can't hit the Carnegie Deli or Junior's on a regular basis, try our approximation. We think it's much better than what we've had in most other parts of the world, and it's fairly healthy to boot. We like to serve these satisfying blintzes with Strawberry Sauce (see opposite) and a dollop of reduced-fat sour cream.

Look for the farmer cheese, a low-fat, dry curd type of cottage cheese, in your supermarket's dairy section.

1 large egg

2 egg whites

2 cups farmer cheese

1/3 cup chopped dried apricots

1 tablespoon pure vanilla extract

1/4 teaspoon ground allspice

12 crepes (page 214)

In a medium bowl, lightly beat the egg and egg whites. Add the cheese, apricots, vanilla, and allspice. Mix well.

Mound a generous 3 tablespoons of the cheese mixture over the bottom third of each crepe, leaving a border all around. Fold the bottom border up over the filling, fold the sides in, and roll up the crepe. Place the filled blintzes on a plate, cover, and refrigerate for at least 30 minutes or up to 6 hours.

Place a heavy-gauge nonstick baking sheet in the oven and preheat the oven to 400F (205C).

Spray the preheated baking sheet with cooking spray. Transfer the blintzes to the baking sheet. Bake in the center of the oven for 5 minutes. Spray the blintzes with cooking spray, then turn them over. Move the sheet to the bottom rack of the oven and bake for about 3 minutes more, until the blintzes are well browned on the bottom.

Strawberry Sauce

This recipe is so simple you can almost make the sauce with one hand while you serve up some blintzes with the other! The sauce is also good with Banana French Toast (page 210) and Strawberry French Toast (page 212).

    1 (10-ounce) package frozen strawberries in syrup, thawed

    1 tablespoon fresh lemon juice

Combine the strawberries in their syrup and the lemon juice in the bowl of a food processor. Process to a smooth puree.

MAKES ABOUT 16 TABLESPOONS

PER TABLESPOON
Fat 0 g
Protein 0 g
Carbohydrates 2 g
Calories 5

SCOTCH EGGS

MAKES 8 SERVINGS

PER SERVING
Fat 4 g
Protein 18 g
Carbohydrates 4 g
Calories 130

Scotch eggs, the old-time bar food of the British Isles, is a favorite of Kevin's from which we've had to work hard to pare the fat grams. We start by cutting the pork in the sausage with turkey and by grinding our own meats rather than buying them preground, because they can contain considerable hidden fat. Use lean pork loin and pieces of turkey breast tenderloin. Trim the meat, cut it into chunks, and grind in a food processor.

The recipe uses both hot and sweet paprika—hot to season the sausage and sweet in the breading. If you can't find hot paprika, use the sweet variety in both and add a pinch of cayenne to the meat mixture. The eggs must be completely dry so that the sausage will stick more easily.

Slice the baked eggs into 6 pieces each, as directed below, and serve about 3 pieces per person (a little Scotch egg goes a long way), atop a bed of lettuce on a platter, around a bowl of Worcestershire sauce for dipping. Scotch eggs can be served warm or at room temperature.

8 ounces ground lean pork

8 ounces ground turkey breast

1 tablespoon poultry seasoning

½ tablespoon hot paprika

2 rusk crackers, broken up

2 tablespoons packed fresh parsley leaves

½ teaspoon sweet paprika

½ teaspoon onion powder

¼ cup all-purpose flour

½ teaspoon salt

¼ teaspoon ground black pepper

2 large egg whites

½ tablespoon water

4 hard-cooked eggs, shelled and wiped very dry

Place a heavy-gauge nonstick baking sheet in the oven and preheat the oven to 450F (230C).

Combine the pork, turkey, poultry seasoning, and hot paprika in a large bowl. Mix thoroughly and set aside.

Combine the crackers, parsley, sweet paprika, and onion powder in the bowl of a food processor. Process to a very fine crumb and transfer the crumbs to a plate. On a second plate, mix together the flour, salt, and pepper. Beat the egg whites and water lightly in a large, shallow bowl.

Roll a hard-cooked egg in the flour to coat. Mold about ½ cup of the sausage all around the egg. Gently roll the sausage-encased egg in the egg white mixture, then in the cracker crumb mixture to coat evenly. Repeat the process with the remaining eggs.

Spray the preheated baking sheet with cooking spray. Carefully transfer the eggs to the baking sheet. Bake for 8 minutes. Turn each egg a little to promote even browning and bake for 4 minutes more. Turn the eggs a little more and bake for about 4 minutes more, until very well browned.

Slice each egg in half lengthwise and then each half crosswise into thirds.

APPLE PANCAKES

MAKES 6 SERVINGS

PER SERVING
Fat 1.5 g
Protein 2 g
Carbohydrates 27 g
Calories 130

For breakfast, for brunch, or for a snack in the middle of the night, for that matter, fruit pancakes are a comforting treat. Serve with syrup or with sour cream or with a little butter and powdered sugar. The pancakes are also good with Apple Chutney (page 265). If you can't find any McIntosh apples, use Jonathans or Galas.

2 McIntosh apples (about 10 ounces total)

2 tablespoons fresh lemon juice

½ cup all-purpose buttermilk baking mix

1 teaspoon baking powder

½ tablespoon ground cinnamon

1 large egg

2 tablespoons golden rum

¼ cup plus 1 tablespoon packed light brown sugar

3 tablespoons water

Place a heavy-gauge nonstick baking sheet in the oven and preheat the oven to 500F (260C).

Peel, core, and chop the apples. Set them aside to soak in a mixture of the lemon juice and ½ cup water.

In a large bowl, mix together the baking mix, baking powder, and cinnamon. In a small bowl, combine the egg, rum, brown sugar, and 3 tablespoons water. Add egg mixture to the dry ingredients. Stir until the mixture is smooth. Drain and fold in the apples.

Spray the preheated baking sheet with cooking spray. Drop 12 pancakes onto the sheet, using about 2 tablespoons of the batter for each. Bake for about 3 minutes, until bubbles begin to appear on the surface of the cakes. Turn them over and bake for about 2 minutes more, until firm and light golden. Serve 2 pancakes per person.

SWEETS

WHEN IT COMES to cutting fat, the proof is not in the pudding. It's in the doughnut . . . and in the cruller . . . and in the beignet . . . and in the fritter—all of those normally deep-fried, fat-laden goodies that most of us eat only on rare occasions these days, if at all. By trading in the vat of fat (no kidding, we've actually seen recipes that start with up to a gallon of oil!) for a hot oven, we've restored "fried" pastries in all their getups—glazed and powdered, filled and coated—to their rightful state.

Although a doughnut cutter can come in handy, you can easily improvise, using a cookie cutter or biscuit cutter or a glass for the outer ring and any small circular object for the inner. By all means save the center scraps for doughnut holes (see page 222). Nutritional counts for most doughnuts (those with a hole in the middle) are based on the doughnut and the doughnut hole that goes with it.

GLAZED CHOCOLATE DOUGHNUTS

MAKES 8 DOUGHNUTS

PER DOUGHNUT
Fat 9 g
Protein 6 g
Carbohydrates 54 g
Calories 310

FORMING AND COATING DOUGHNUT HOLES

Some people like these tender mouthfuls even more than the doughnuts from which they're left over. Remove the little circles of dough from the center of the doughnut cutter (or from whatever implement you are using to cut out the centers of the doughnuts). Roll each into a ball, as you would form a meatball. Float the holes in a shallow bowl filled with the egg white wash, then remove gently to a second shallow bowl filled with the crumb mixture. Shake and rotate the bowl to coat the holes with crumbs. (The holes are too fragile to roll in the crumbs.) Remove to the baking sheet with the doughnuts and bake.

Long ago—in another time, another place, and another life— Barry used to hang out mornings, when he was visiting a friend in Houston, at a local truck stop known for its doughnuts. Frequented mostly by truckers and cops, the joint made just about the greatest doughnuts in the world, which were invariably sold out by 7 A.M.

This doughnut, which is pretty terrific in its own right, if we do say so ourselves, reminds Barry of the glazed chocolate doughnuts they used to sell at his Texas truck stop. It represents the essence of what this book is all about. We have here a fabulous doughnut with all the taste, richness, and satisfaction of the high-fat, fried, commercial kind, but only a fraction of the fat and none of the mess (which is another reason few people attempt doughnuts at home these days). Doughnuts are no harder to make than biscuits, but the frying process seems to leave a layer of grease on all surfaces in the near vicinity.

We don't know what the doughnuts at that Houston truck stop of yore weighed in at, but a 2-ounce chocolate cake doughnut at Dunkin Donuts has 14 grams of fat. Compare that with 9 grams for our 3½-ounce beauty!

2¼ cups all-purpose flour

1 tablespoon baking powder

1 teaspoon baking soda

½ teaspoon salt

½ teaspoon ground cinnamon

¾ cup granulated sugar

1 large egg

2 tablespoons unsalted butter, melted

2 ounces unsweetened chocolate, melted

½ tablespoon pure vanilla extract

½ cup buttermilk

2 large egg whites, lightly beaten with 1 teaspoon water

⅓ cup chocolate wafer crumbs (about 15 wafers)

½ cup confectioners' sugar

1½ tablespoons water

Preheat the oven to 400F (205C).

Sift the flour, baking powder, baking soda, salt, and cinnamon together into a mixing bowl. In a large bowl, combine the granulated sugar, egg, butter, melted chocolate, and vanilla. Whisk until light and frothy. Alternately stir in the flour mixture and the buttermilk in thirds, to form a very stiff dough.

On a floured work surface, pat the dough into an about ½-inch-thick 9-inch circle. Cut out 8 doughnuts with a 2¾-inch doughnut cutter. Using a pastry brush, paint each doughnut all over with the egg white and water wash, then roll to coat in the wafer crumbs. (Reroll holes, or follow instructions on page 222 for doughnut holes.)

Place the doughnuts on a heavy-gauge nonstick baking sheet and spray each lightly with cooking spray. Bake for 10 to 12 minutes, until puffed and firm. Meanwhile, combine the confectioners' sugar and the 1½ tablespoons water in a shallow bowl and whisk thoroughly for a glaze. While the doughnuts are still warm, dip them into the glaze.

LEMON CRULLERS

MAKES 12 CRULLERS

PER CRULLER
Fat 2 g
Protein 4 g
Carbohydrates 33 g
Calories 170

We use yeast instead of the usual baking powder because it produces a lighter and airier cruller. Our long twists, however, are of a more traditional shape than the twisted circles we've been seeing of late. For an even stronger lemon flavor, substitute ½ cup of lemon wafer crumbs for the vanilla crumbs.

1 teaspoon plus ¼ cup granulated sugar

⅓ cup lukewarm water (105 to 115F; 40 to 45C)

2¼ teaspoons (1 envelope) quick-rise yeast

⅓ cup skim milk

2½ cups all-purpose flour

1 teaspoon grated lemon zest

1 teaspoon ground cinnamon

½ teaspoon salt

1 large egg, lightly beaten

2 egg whites, lightly beaten with 1 teaspoon water

½ cup vanilla wafer crumbs (about 18 wafers)

⅓ cup confectioners' sugar

Dissolve the 1 teaspoon granulated sugar in the lukewarm water. Stir in the yeast and set aside to proof until bubbly, 8 to 10 minutes.

In a small saucepan over medium heat, scald the milk until just bubbling around the edge, 5 to 6 minutes. Remove from the heat, add the remaining ¼ cup granulated sugar, and stir until completely dissolved. Allow to cool to room temperature.

Combine the flour, lemon zest, cinnamon, and salt in the bowl of a food processor and process until combined, 1 minute. Scrape in the yeast mixture. With the machine running, add the egg through the feed tube, then add the cooled milk mixture slowly just until a dough ball forms.

Remove the dough to a ceramic or glass bowl that has been

lightly sprayed with cooking spray. Cover tightly with plastic wrap and set aside in a draft-free place until doubled in size, 30 to 40 minutes.

On a floured work surface, pat the dough into a ½-inch-thick 9 × 8-inch rectangle. Cut the rectangle into 12 (8 × ¾-inch) strips. Brush the strips with the egg white wash and roll to coat in the wafer crumbs. Grasp each strip at both ends and rotate the ends 2 or 3 times in opposite directions to create a twisted shape. Place on a heavy-gauge nonstick baking sheet that has been lightly sprayed with cooking spray. Push the ends of the strips down on the pan. Cover and set aside to rise until the sticks have doubled in size and the dough no longer springs back to the touch, about 30 minutes.

Preheat the oven to 400F (205C).

Bake until golden, 10 to 12 minutes. Dip the top of each cruller in the confectioners' sugar to coat.

OLD-FASHIONED DOUGHNUTS

MAKE 8 DOUGHNUTS

PER DOUGHNUT
Fat 5 g
Protein 5 g
Carbohydrates 45 g
Calories 240

There's nothing quite like the taste of a real old-fashioned doughnut—simple, yet so eminently satisfying! In this svelte update, the combination of melted butter and breadcrumbs lends baked doughnuts a richness and flakiness until now always associated with deep-frying. Be sure to use unsalted butter and unflavored breadcrumbs.

DRESSING YOUR DOUGHNUTS

For their coating, many doughnuts are immersed first in a liquid (egg, milk, or melted butter) and then in a crumb mixture of some sort. Put the liquid in a shallow bowl. Although we often scatter breading mixtures on a plate, it is easier to coat a doughnut if the crumbs are placed into a shallow bowl. Float the doughnut in the liquid and paint it all over with the egg or milk. Gently transfer the doughnut to the bowl of crumbs. Push the crumbs up through the center to coat the inside of the circle and up the sides to coat the outside. Sprinkle crumbs over the top and carefully remove the doughnut to the baking sheet.

2 cups all-purpose flour

1 tablespoon baking powder

1 teaspoon baking soda

½ teaspoon salt

½ teaspoon ground cinnamon

½ cup granulated sugar

2 large egg whites or 1 large egg, lightly beaten

4 tablespoons unsalted butter, melted

½ cup buttermilk

½ cup breadcrumbs

¼ cup confectioners' sugar

Preheat the oven to 400F (205C)

Sift the flour, baking powder, baking soda, salt, and cinnamon together into a medium bowl. In a large bowl, combine the granulated sugar, egg whites, and 2 tablespoons of the butter. Whisk until light and frothy. Alternately whisk in the flour mixture and the buttermilk in thirds, to form a very stiff dough.

On a lightly floured work surface, pat the dough into a 9-inch circle, about ½ inch thick. Cut out 8 doughnuts with a 2¾-inch doughnut cutter. Using a pastry brush, paint each doughnut all over with some of the remaining melted butter, then roll to coat in breadcrumbs.

Place the doughnuts on a heavy-gauge nonstick baking sheet and spray each lightly with cooking spray. Bake until puffed and golden, 10 to 12 minutes. While still warm, dip the top of each doughnut in the confectioners' sugar.

GRAHAM CRACKER BEIGNETS

MAKES 24 BEIGNETS

PER BEIGNET
Fat 2.5 g
Protein 2 g
Carbohydrates 17 g
Calories 100

The best-known beignets ("beignet" is French for fritter) are served with café au lait at the Café du Monde in the French Quarter. Just like their New Orleans inspiration, ours are best hot out of the oven and accompanied by thick, rich coffee. The whole-wheat flour adds an earthy dimension to the pastries that is heightened and complemented by the graham cracker coating.

1 teaspoon plus ⅓ cup sugar

⅓ cup lukewarm water (105 to 115F; 40 to 45C)

1 tablespoon active dry yeast

1⅓ cups all-purpose flour

1⅓ cups whole-wheat flour

½ teaspoon salt

1 large egg, lightly beaten

½ cup buttermilk, at room temperature

3 tablespoons canola oil

¾ cup graham cracker crumbs

½ cup confectioners' sugar

Dissolve the 1 teaspoon sugar in the lukewarm water. Stir in the yeast and set aside to proof until bubbly, 8 to 10 minutes.

Combine the flours, the remaining ⅓ cup sugar, and the salt in the bowl of a food processor. Process until combined, 1 minute. Scrape in the yeast mixture. With the machine running, add the egg through the feed tube, then the buttermilk. After a dough ball forms, continue to process for 1 minute more to knead.

Remove the dough to a ceramic or glass bowl that has been lightly sprayed with cooking spray. Turn the ball in the bowl to coat. Cover tightly with plastic wrap and set aside in a draft-free place until the dough has doubled in size and no longer springs back to the touch, about 1 hour.

Pour the canola oil into a large, shallow bowl. Sprinkle the graham cracker crumbs on a plate. Remove the dough to a work surface and pat it into a ½-inch-thick, 12 × 7-inch rectangle. Cut the rectangle into 24 (3½ × 1-inch) strips. Dip each strip into the oil, then turn in the cracker crumbs to coat. Place the strips on a heavy-gauge nonstick baking sheet, cover, and let rise for 30 minutes.

Preheat the oven to 400F (205C).

Bake for 10 to 11 minutes, until the beignets are golden and firm to the touch.

WHOLE-WHEAT DOUGHNUTS

MAKES 12 DOUGHNUTS

PER DOUGHNUT
Fat 4.5 g
Protein 7 g
Carbohydrates 34 g
Calories 200

This recipe works equally well using graham cracker crumbs in lieu of the wheat germ, although it will produce a doughnut with a slightly less crunchy coating than the wheat germ rendition. We also like to experiment with some of the flavored graham crackers, such as honey-cinnamon.

If you don't have a doughnut cutter, (they're not as prevalent as they once were—look for one in a restaurant supply store or at a flea market), cut the dough circles out with a 3-inch-diameter biscuit cutter or glass. Use any 1-inch circular object to cut out the hole.

2 cups all-purpose flour

1 cup whole-wheat flour

1 tablespoon baking powder

½ tablespoon baking soda

½ teaspoon salt

¾ teaspoon ground nutmeg

½ cup granulated sugar

2 large eggs

3 tablespoons unsalted butter, melted

¾ cup buttermilk

¾ cup wheat germ

2 egg whites

1 tablespoon water

2 tablespoons confectioners' sugar

In a medium bowl, mix together the flours, baking powder, baking soda, salt, and nutmeg. In a large bowl, combine the granulated sugar, the eggs, and the butter. Whisk until light and frothy. Alternately stir in the flour mixture and the buttermilk, in thirds, to form a very stiff dough. Cover and refrigerate for 30 minutes.

Preheat the oven to 400F (250C).

Scatter the wheat germ on a plate. In a large, shallow bowl, beat the egg whites with the water. On a lightly floured work surface, pat the dough into an about ½-inch-thick 10-inch circle. Cut out 12 doughnuts with a 2¾-inch doughnut cutter. Paint each doughnut all over with the egg white wash, then roll it to coat in the wheat germ. Place the doughnuts on a heavy-gauge nonstick baking sheet and spray with cooking spray.

Bake for 10 to 11 minutes, until the doughnuts puff up and turn golden brown. While the doughnuts are still warm, sift the confectioners' sugar over them.

PLANTAIN COCONUT FRITTERS

MAKES 16 FRITTERS

PER FRITTER
Fat 2.5 g
Protein 2 g
Carbohydrates 18 g
Calories 100

Evocative of the Caribbean, this fritter contains pieces of chopped plantain coated with a thick coconut batter and dropped onto a baking sheet instead of into a skillet of fat. Use a very ripe plantain, one that is fairly soft and black, or "maduro," instead of green or yellow. Be sure to use light coconut milk, which has quite a bit less fat. Glaze the fritters while they are still warm, so that the glaze will cook lightly on the doughnuts, creating a shell as it cools.

1 very ripe plantain

½ cup plus 1½ tablespoons light coconut milk

2 large eggs, lightly beaten

1 cup sweetened coconut flakes

1 cup all-purpose flour

¼ cup granulated sugar

1 teaspoon baking powder

1 teaspoon ground cinnamon

1½ cup confectioners' sugar

Peel and slice the plantain into ¼-inch rounds, then quarter each round. Combine the plantain in a small bowl with the ½ cup coconut milk and set aside for about 20 minutes.

Place a heavy-gauge nonstick baking sheet in the oven and preheat the oven to 450F (230C).

To the plantain and coconut milk mixture, add the eggs, coconut flakes, flour, granulated sugar, baking powder, and cinnamon. Mix well.

Spray the preheated baking sheet with cooking spray. Drop 16 fritters onto the sheet, using about 2 tablespoons of the batter for each and leaving about 1 inch of space between fritters. Lightly spray fritters with cooking spray. Bake for 7 minutes. Spray the fritters again, turn, and bake about 7 minutes more, until golden.

For a glaze, mix together the confectioners' sugar and the remaining 1½ tablespoons coconut milk in a small bowl. Remove the fritters to a wire rack placed over a sheet of wax paper. While still warm from the oven, paint the fritters with the glaze.

BANANA DOUGHNUTS

MAKES 13 DOUGHNUTS

PER DOUGHNUT
Fat 3 g
Protein 4 g
Carbohydrates 35 g
Calories 180

For variety, we sometimes replace the graham cracker crumbs in which these doughnuts are rolled with an equal amount of vanilla wafer crumbs, chocolate wafer crumbs, or wheat germ, which gives a crunchier coating. If you've been really good and deserve a splurge, combine ½ cup graham cracker crumbs and ½ cup chopped walnuts in a food processor and process to a fine grind.

2½ cups all-purpose flour

2 teaspoons baking powder

1 teaspoon baking soda

½ teaspoon salt

¼ teaspoon ground nutmeg

½ cup granulated sugar

1 large egg

2 egg whites

2 tablespoons unsalted butter, melted

⅓ cup buttermilk

1 teaspoon pure vanilla extract

1 banana, mashed

½ tablespoon water

¾ cup graham cracker crumbs

⅓ cup confectioners' sugar

Preheat the oven to 400F (205C).

Whisk the flour, baking powder, baking soda, salt, and nutmeg together in a medium bowl. In a large bowl, combine the granulated sugar, egg, 1 of the egg whites, the butter, buttermilk, and vanilla. Whisk until the mixture is light and frothy. Whisk in the banana. Stir in the flour mixture to form a stiff dough.

On a floured work surface, pat the dough into an about ½-inch-thick 12 × 8-inch rectangle with well-floured hands. With a well-floured 2¾-inch doughnut cutter, cut out 11 doughnuts. Gather the scraps and cut out 2 additional doughnuts.

In a large, shallow bowl, whisk the remaining egg white with the water. Scatter the graham cracker crumbs on a plate. Paint each doughnut all over with the egg white wash, then roll to coat in the cracker crumbs.

Place the doughnuts on a heavy-gauge nonstick baking sheet and spray each lightly with cooking spray. Bake for 10 to 12 minutes, until puffed and golden. While still warm, dip the top of each doughnut in the confectioners' sugar.

CINNAMON-APPLE-RAISIN PILLOWS

MAKES 8 PILLOWS

PER PILLOW
Fat 2 g
Protein 3 g
Carbohydrates 39 g
Calories 190

**We created these cookielike pastries with apple fritters in mind.
And they have the taste and texture of an apple fritter—close
your eyes, and that is precisely what you will think you are eating. However, they look more like a fried cookie, so we've called
them pillows instead of fritters. Don't substitute another variety
of apple for the readily available Granny Smith, whose firmness
and flavor are perfect for this recipe.**

1 Granny Smith apple

1 tablespoon fresh lemon juice

1/3 cup golden raisins

2 tablespoons golden rum

1 1/3 cups all-purpose buttermilk baking mix

1/3 cup packed dark brown sugar

1/2 tablespoon baking powder

3/4 teaspoon ground cinnamon

1/2 teaspoon salt

1/8 teaspoon ground nutmeg

1 large egg

1/2 cup buttermilk

1/2 teaspoon pure vanilla extract

1/2 cup confectioners' sugar

1 1/2 tablespoons water

Place a heavy-gauge nonstick baking sheet in the oven and preheat
the oven to 400F (250C).

Peel, core, and dice the apple, then toss it with the lemon juice.
Combine the raisins and rum in a small bowl and set aside to soak.
In another small bowl, mix together the baking mix, brown sugar,
baking powder, cinnamon, salt, and nutmeg.

In a large bowl, whisk together the egg, buttermilk, and vanilla. Add the apple and raisins, along with their soaking liquid. Slowly stir in the flour mixture and set aside for about 5 minutes.

Spray the preheated baking sheet with cooking spray. Drop 8 pillows onto the baking sheet, using about ⅓ cup of the batter for each. Spray them lightly with cooking spray. Bake for 12 to 14 minutes, until they have begun to brown. Meanwhile, combine the confectioners' sugar and water in a small bowl for a glaze. Stir until smooth.

Remove the pillows to a wire rack placed over a sheet of wax paper. Brush with the glaze and allow to cool completely.

JELLY DOUGHNUTS

MAKES 9 DOUGHNUTS

PER DOUGHNUT
Fat 4.5 g
Protein 9 g
Carbohydrates 75 g
Calories 380

We've simplified jelly doughnut making considerably by encasing the filling between layers of dough before the doughnut bakes rather than piping it into a cooked doughnut. This method works best if you use pastry filling, which can be found in the baking section of your supermarket. It is thicker and less sugary than jelly. Vary the flavor by substituting strawberry or apricot filling for the raspberry, but do use the thicker product.

1 teaspoon plus ¾ cup sugar

¼ cup lukewarm water (105 to 115F; 40 to 45C)

1½ tablespoons (2 envelopes) active dry yeast

⅔ cup skim milk

2 tablespoons unsalted butter

4 cups all-purpose flour

2 teaspoons grated orange zest

1 teaspoon salt

2 large eggs, lightly beaten

9 tablespoons seedless raspberry pastry filling

1 egg white, lightly beaten

½ cup breadcrumbs

¼ cup confectioners' sugar

Dissolve 1 teaspoon of the sugar in the lukewarm water. Stir in the yeast and set aside to proof until bubbly, 8 to 10 minutes.

In a small saucepan over medium heat, scald the milk until just bubbling around the edge, 5 to 6 minutes. Remove from the heat, add the remaining ¾ cup sugar and the butter, and stir until the sugar has completely dissolved. Allow to cool to room temperature.

Combine the flour, orange zest, and salt in the bowl of a food processor, and process until combined, 1 minute. Scrape in the yeast mixture. With the machine running, add the whole eggs through the feed tube. Pour in the milk mixture and process until a dough ball forms.

Remove the dough to a ceramic or glass bowl that has been lightly sprayed with cooking spray. Cover tightly with plastic wrap and set aside in a draft-free place until doubled in size, about 45 minutes.

Cut the dough in half. On a floured work surface, roll each half into a ⅛-inch-thick 14-inch circle. Using a 3-inch cookie or biscuit cutter, cut out 18 circles. Mound 1 tablespoon of the raspberry filling in the center of each of 9 of the circles. Paint the outer edges around the filling with egg white. Top with the remaining 9 circles, crimp the edges together very tightly to seal, and paint the exposed dough with egg white. Coat each doughnut on each side with breadcrumbs. Place on a heavy-gauge nonstick baking sheet that has been sprayed lightly with cooking spray. Cover loosely with a clean dish towel and set aside to rise until doubled in size, about 1 hour.

Preheat the oven to 400F (205C).

Bake for 8 to 10 minutes, until the doughnuts are puffed and golden. Remove the doughnuts from the oven and dip the tops in the confectioners' sugar.

Variation

Should you want to experiment with the somewhat more involved traditional method, you will need to roll and cut out only 9 dough circles, each ¼ inch thick. After the doughnuts have baked, poke a hole in the side and pipe the filling in through a pastry bag fitted with a small nozzle. With this method, you can use jelly or jam, but choose one with a smooth consistency rather than a chunky preserve that would clog the nozzle of the pastry bag.

CHOCOLATE BANANA WONTONS

MAKES 15 WONTONS

PER WONTON
Fat 1.5 g
Protein 1 g
Carbohydrates 9 g
Calories 50

Packed with banana, pecans, and chocolate chips, you just have to love these! We like to serve them either with assorted fruit and a fondue of apricot all-fruit thinned with a bit of apricot brandy, or with Crispy Chocolate Cherry Ravioli (page 242) and a fondue of orange marmalade cut with a bit of orange liqueur.

1 firm, ripe banana

2 tablespoons chopped pecans

2 tablespoons mini chocolate chips

1 tablespoon dark brown sugar

15 square wonton skins

Place a heavy-gauge nonstick baking sheet in the oven and preheat the oven to 475F (245C).

Peel the banana and cut it into ¼-inch dice. In a medium bowl, mix together the banana, pecans, chocolate chips, and brown sugar. Mound 2 teaspoons of the mixture in the center of each wonton. Moisten 2 adjoining edges of the skin with water, fold over the filling to form a triangle, and press down along the edges to seal closed.

Spray the preheated baking sheet to coat lightly with cooking spray. Place the wontons on the sheet and spray each lightly with cooking spray. Bake for 3 minutes, turn, and bake about 2 minutes more, until golden and crisp.

Variation: Chocolate Banana Firecrackers

For a really festive presentation, assemble the wontons as little rolled-up firecrackers. Instead of mounding the filling in the center of each wonton and folding it over to seal, mound the filling toward one edge. Moisten the other three edges with water and roll the skin into a cigar shape around the filling, starting with the edge next to the filling. Pinch and twist the ends closed.

CRISPY CHOCOLATE CHERRY RAVIOLI

MAKES 12 RAVIOLI

PER RAVIOLI
Fat 1.5 g
Protein 9 g
Carbohydrates 28 g
Calories 160

These elegant and unusual pastries would be perfect on a dessert buffet or plated and served with tea, especially if drizzled with a little of our fat-free Créme Anglaise (see opposite) The use of wonton skins in a dessert may sound a little strange, but they work beautifully, eliminating both the time and fat involved in most pastry doughs. Sugared and baked, they turn wonderfully crisp.

2 cups skim-milk ricotta cheese

1 cup confectioners' sugar plus extra for dusting

½ cup diced dried sweet or sour cherries

¼ cup mini chocolate chips

1 teaspoon pure vanilla extract

24 square wonton skins

Place a heavy-gauge nonstick baking sheet in the oven and preheat the oven to 450F (230C).

Combine the ricotta, the 1 cup confectioners' sugar, cherries, chocolate chips, and vanilla in a medium bowl. Mix thoroughly.

Mound ¼ cup of the filling in the center of each of 12 wontons. Moisten the edges all around with water. Put a second skin on top of each and press around the edges to seal.

Spray the preheated baking sheet with cooking spray. Place the wontons on the sheet and spray them lightly. Bake for 3 minutes, turn, and bake until very crispy and well browned, about 3 minutes more. Sift confectioners' sugar over the ravioli.

Crème Anglaise

Perfect not only for topping our Crispy Chocolate Cherry Ravioli (see opposite), this svelte rendition also works well with the Chocolate Banana Wontons (page 240).

(see opposite)

½ cup skim milk

1 large egg

2 tablespoons sugar

½ teaspoon almond extract

Put the milk into a small saucepan and heat over low heat until it just begins to steam.

In a medium bowl, whisk the egg and sugar until blended. Slowly whisk in the warm milk. Return the milk mixture to the saucepan. Cook, stirring constantly, until slightly thickened, 3 to 4 minutes. Whisk in the almond extract.

MAKES ABOUT 12
TABLESPOONS

PER TABLESPOON
Fat 0 g
Protein 1 g
Carbohydrates 3 g
Calories 20

SUGAR AND CINNAMON PLANTAIN CRISPS

MAKES 24 CRISPS

PER CRISP
Fat 0 g
Protein 0 g
Carbohydrates 5 g
Calories 15

Plantains are sold in Latin, Caribbean, and African markets, and are carried by many urban supermarkets. Choose a yellow plantain for this recipe, one that has ripened more than a firm green plantain but is not yet as soft as one that has turned black.

These are simple, comforting sweets that appeal to children and to the child in all of us. They resemble cookies, and we think of them as sort of Latin American snickerdoodles.

> 1 ripe plantain
>
> ¼ cup sugar
>
> 1 teaspoon ground cinnamon

Place a heavy-gauge nonstick baking sheet in the oven and preheat the oven to 500F (260C).

Peel and slice the plantain on the diagonal into ¼-inch-thick rounds. Combine the plantain in a plastic bag with the sugar and cinnamon, and shake to coat well.

Place the rounds on the baking sheet and bake for 3 minutes. Turn and bake for about 3 minutes more, until crisp. As soon as the crisps have cooled enough to handle, return them to the plastic bag and shake once more in the sugar and cinnamon.

MEXICAN SUGAR COOKIES

The old-fashioned, family-run neighborhood Mexican restaurant on Chicago's North Side that Kevin has been frequenting for 20-odd years hosts a popular Sunday brunch. The steam tables hold dozens of tempting entrées, and there's even a tureen of menudo, but without fail Barry heads straight for El Jardin's dessert bar first and piles his plate with the sugar cookies, called *buñuelos*. They are normally high in fat, and we've even seen so-called healthy recipes weighing in at over 5 grams of fat per cookie—compared with our 1.5 grams.

In traditional Latin American fashion, you could heat about 2 tablespoons honey until just liquid enough to be pourable, about 45 seconds, on HIGH power in the microwave, and drizzle it over the *buñuelos*. The cookies are also good with vanilla frozen yogurt or ice cream.

¼ cup sugar

½ tablespoon ground cinnamon

2 (about 8-inch) flour tortillas

Preheat the oven to 450F (230C).

Mix the sugar and cinnamon together on a plate. Spray the tortillas on both sides with cooking spray. Press both sides of each tortilla into the sugar and cinnamon mixture to coat.

Place on a heavy-gauge nonstick baking sheet and bake for 2 minutes. Turn and bake for 2 to 3 minutes more, until crisp and dark brown. Break each tortilla into 4 cookies.

MAKES 8 COOKIES

PER COOKIE
Fat 1.5 g
Protein 2 g
Carbohydrates 17 g
Calories 80

SAUCES

FRIED FOODS ARE all too often served with sauces that are as
outlandishly high in fat as the dishes they accompany. Bearing in
mind that it would be rather silly to trim a dish down to its ideal
weight and then slather on a topping that puts back much of the
fat saved by not deep-frying, we set out to solve the sauce problem. This is not to say that there is anything wrong with the occasional pat of succulent butter or dollop of ethereal whipped cream,
just that full-fat products should be savored, and often represent
nothing more than wasted fat grams in a sauce.

We use reduced-fat mayonnaise to make low-fat tartars and
aïolis, whip up low-fat cream sauces with reduced-fat sour cream,
and create lots of flavorful Asian dipping sauces and robust salsas
that are virtually fat-free.

Green Tomato Tartar

Cherry Tomato Tartar

Pepper Tartar

Tomato Garlic Aïoli

Cayenne Mayonnaise

Cumin Mayonnaise

Creole Mustard Aïoli

**Apricot Mustard Dipping
Sauce**

Soy Dipping Sauce

Hoisin Dipping Sauce

Ginger Dipping Sauce

Mango Lime Salsa

Mixed Pepper Salsa

**Corn and Orange Tomato
Salsa**

Wasabi Cream

Caper Cream

Horseradish Cream

Apple Chutney

Tomato Broth

GREEN TOMATO TARTAR

MAKES ABOUT 1 CUP
(16 TABLESPOONS)

PER TABLESPOON
Fat 0.5 g
Protein 0 g
Carbohydrates 1 g
Calories 10

We never tire of green tomatoes, well dressed here in a citrus-tasting mayonnaise spiked with paprika. It provides a nice finishing touch for Smoked Turkey Hush Puppies (page 74), Louisiana Crawfish Cakes (page 119), or Cajun Catfish (page 126).

1 small green tomato, diced (about ¾ cup)

¼ cup reduced-fat mayonnaise

2 tablespoons fresh lemon juice

1 tablespoon chopped fresh parsley

½ teaspoon paprika

½ teaspoon salt

¼ teaspoon ground black pepper

¼ teaspoon grated lemon zest

Combine the tomato and mayonnaise in a small bowl and toss to coat the tomato. Add the lemon juice, parsley, paprika, salt, pepper, and lemon zest. Mix thoroughly.

CHERRY TOMATO TARTAR

A touch of pungent Cajun spice adds an interesting flavor dimension to this straightforward tomato and bell pepper–dotted mayonnaise mixture. Serve it with Italian-Style Fried Clams (page 118), Cajun Crab and Corn Beignets (page 104), or Cornmeal-Coated Catfish Nuggets (page 136).

MAKES ABOUT 1 CUP
(16 TABLESPOONS)

PER TABLESPOON
Fat 1 g
Protein 0 g
Carbohydrates 1 g
Calories 15

8 cherry tomatoes

½ cup reduced-fat mayonnaise

1 tablespoon fresh lemon juice

¼ teaspoon Cajun seasoning (prepared or page 24)

¼ teaspoon salt

⅛ teaspoon ground black pepper

¼ cup finely diced green bell pepper

Quarter each cherry tomato and then cut each quarter in half.

Put the mayonnaise in a small bowl. Mix in the lemon juice. Stir in the Cajun seasoning, salt, and black pepper. Fold in the tomatoes and bell pepper.

PEPPER TARTAR

MAKES ABOUT 14
TABLESPOONS

PER TABLESPOON
Fat 1.5 g
Protein 0 g
Carbohydrates 1 g
Calories 20

Serve this mild tartar with Spicy Smelts (page 146) or Cajun Crab and Corn Beignets (page 104). Look for the sweet cherry peppers (which, despite their name, do have a bit of a bite) in jars in your supermarket's Italian aisle. If you can't find any, use jarred pepperoncini instead.

6 sweet cherry peppers

½ cup reduced-fat mayonnaise

2 tablespoons fresh lemon juice

1 tablespoon chopped fresh parsley

½ teaspoon lemon pepper

Seed and chop the peppers.

Combine the peppers, mayonnaise, lemon juice, parsley, and lemon pepper in a small bowl. Mix well.

TOMATO GARLIC AÏOLI

Our tomato-accented rendition of the classic garlic mayonnaise of Provence is a natural with Cayenne Popcorn Calamari (page 102), Chicken Nuggets (page 87), or Salt Cod and Potato Cakes (page 140).

MAKES ABOUT
18 TABLESPOONS

PER TABLESPOON
Fat 2 g
Protein 0 g
Carbohydrates 1 g
Calories 25

1 cup reduced-fat mayonnaise

2 tablespoons tomato paste

2 cloves garlic, crushed

Mix the mayonnaise, tomato paste, and garlic together well in a small bowl.

CAYENNE MAYONNAISE

MAKES ABOUT
9 TABLESPOONS

PER TABLESPOON
Fat 2 g
Protein 0 g
Carbohydrates 1 g
Calories 25

Simple and spicy, this makes a smashing accompaniment to Classic Maryland Crab Cakes (page 98) or Oyster Po'boys (page 123).

½ cup reduced-fat mayonnaise

1 tablespoon minced fresh parsley

½ teaspoon grated lemon zest

¼ teaspoon cayenne pepper

¼ teaspoon ground black pepper

Combine the mayonnaise, parsley, lemon zest, cayenne, and black pepper in a small bowl. Mix thoroughly.

CUMIN MAYONNAISE

The prevailing influence in this recipe is robust, aromatic cumin, making the sauce a natural pairing for its Middle Eastern neighbor, Pita Pocket Chips (page 188). We also like to serve it with Savory Turkey Pastries (page 78), Key West Sweet Potato and Conch Fritters (page 120), or Clam and Pepper Fritters (page 112).

½ cup reduced-fat mayonnaise

3 tablespoons fresh lime juice

2 teaspoons ground cumin

Salt, to taste

Ground black pepper, to taste

Mix the mayonnaise, lime juice, cumin, salt, and pepper together in a small bowl.

MAKES ABOUT ¾ CUP
(12 TABLESPOONS)

PER TABLESPOON
Fat 1.5 g
Protein 0 g
Carbohydrates 1 g
Calories 20

CREOLE MUSTARD AÏOLI

MAKES ABOUT ½ CUP
(8 TABLESPOONS)

PER TABLESPOON
Fat 1.5 g
Protein 0 g
Carbohydrates 1 g
Calories 25

What would you serve with Creole Okra (page 177)? Why, of course, Creole Mustard Aïoli. We also like it with Cajun Catfish (page 126).

¼ cup plus 2 tablespoons reduced-fat mayonnaise

1½ tablespoons Dijon mustard

½ tablespoon fresh lemon juice

½ tablespoon Creole seasoning (prepared or page 25)

Combine the mayonnaise, mustard, lemon juice, and Creole seasoning in a small bowl and mix together well.

APRICOT MUSTARD DIPPING SAUCE

The mixture of fiery Chinese mustard and soothing apricot jam proves just the right combination to bring out the best in a range of nibbles, including Rock Shrimp Spring Rolls (page 106), Crusty Country Ribs (page 46), and Chili-Spiked Turkey Wontons (page 72). Look for the Chinese mustard in your market's Asian section or stockpile the little envelopes of the stuff that come with Chinese take-out.

MAKES ABOUT
9 TABLESPOONS

PER TABLESPOON
Fat 0 g
Protein 0 g
Carbohydrates 9 g
Calories 35

¼ cup plus 2 tablespoons fruit-sweetened apricot preserves

2 tablespoons Chinese mustard

1½ tablespoons hot tap water

Mix the apricot preserves, mustard, and water together in a small bowl.

SOY DIPPING SAUCE

**MAKES ABOUT
6 TABLESPOONS**

PER TABLESPOON
Fat 0 g
Protein 0 g
Carbohydrates 2 g
Calories 15

**The orangy, slightly salty tang of Soy Dipping Sauce comple-
ments Chili-Spiked Turkey Wontons (page 72) perfectly. It's
also quite good with Coconut Porcupine Prawns (page 105).**

3 tablespoons reduced-sodium soy sauce

2 tablespoons rice vinegar

½ teaspoon sesame oil

½ tablespoon grated fresh ginger

2 teaspoons sugar

1 teaspoon grated orange zest

Combine the soy sauce, vinegar, and sesame oil in a small bowl. Mix
in the ginger, sugar, and orange zest.

HOISIN DIPPING SAUCE

Hoisin sauce, sold in many supermarkets as well as in Asian groceries, provides a touch of cooling sweetness to temper the spiciness of such dishes as Peanut-Covered Wings (page 88) and Chili-Spiked Turkey Wontons (page 72). It also works nicely with Crusty Country Ribs (page 46). For this sauce, choose the thinner hoisin that comes in a plastic squeeze-bottle over the more pastelike variety in a glass jar.

¾ cup hoisin sauce

¼ cup reduced-sodium soy sauce

1 tablespoon rice vinegar

½ tablespoon sesame oil

2 tablespoons chopped fresh cilantro

Combine the hoisin sauce, soy sauce, rice vinegar, and sesame oil in a small bowl. Add the cilantro and mix well.

MAKES ABOUT 1 CUP
(16 TABLESPOONS)

PER TABLESPOON
Fat 1 g
Protein 1 g
Carbohydrates 6 g
Calories 30

GINGER DIPPING SAUCE

MAKES ABOUT 1 CUP
(16 TABLESPOONS)

PER TABLESPOON
Fat 0 g
Protein 1 g
Carbohydrates 2 g
Calories 10

Soy sauce defines the sassy, salty character of this sauce, while hoisin sauce and sugar give a touch of sweetness, and cilantro and ginger spice things up a bit. Try it with Beef and Spinach Goyza (page 36), Chili-Spiked Turkey Wontons (page 72), or Fish Toast Triangles (page 138).

½ cup plus 1 tablespoon reduced-sodium soy sauce

1½ tablespoons hoisin sauce

1½ tablespoons rice vinegar

2 tablespoons chopped fresh cilantro

1½ tablespoons grated fresh ginger

½ tablespoon snipped chives

½ tablespoon sugar

1 large clove garlic, minced.

Combine the soy sauce, hoisin sauce, and rice vinegar in a medium bowl. Mix in the cilantro, ginger, chives, sugar, and garlic.

MANGO LIME SALSA

Cool and tropical, but boasting a goodly amount of cilantro and jalapeño, Mango Lime Salsa is a complex delight. Kevin has been known to devour a bowl of it all by itself, but you may prefer to serve it up with Coconut Porcupine Prawns (page 105), Blue Corn–Coated Plantain Coins (page 166), or Tequila Scallops (page 114).

1 medium mango (about 1 pound)

½ cup diced green bell pepper

⅓ cup diced red onion

2 tablespoons chopped fresh cilantro

½ tablespoon minced jalapeño chile

¼ teaspoon grated lime zest

2 tablespoons fresh lime juice

Peel, seed, and dice the mango.

In a medium bowl, combine the mango, bell pepper, onion, cilantro, jalapeño chile, and lime zest. Add the lime juice and toss to mix.

MAKES ABOUT 2 CUPS
(32 TABLESPOONS)

PER TABLESPOON
Fat 0 g
Protein 0 g
Carbohydrates 1 g
Calories 5

MIXED PEPPER SALSA

MAKES ABOUT 4 CUPS
(64 TABLESPOONS)

PER TABLESPOON
Fat 0 g
Protein 0 g
Carbohydrates 0 g
Calories 0

A cornucopia of sweet and hot peppers gives this salsa complexity and character. Try it with Blue Corn–Coated Plantain Coins (page 166), Pita Pocket Chips (page 188), or Caribbean Plantain Chips (page 165). We use it in our Breakfast Burrito (page 202) and usually serve extra on the side. In fact, we like it so much we always make a big batch.

2 large plum tomatoes

1 jalapeño chile

1 banana pepper

1 green bell pepper

1 yellow bell pepper

1 small yellow onion

½ cup chopped fresh cilantro

3 tablespoons fresh lime juice

Dice the tomatoes. Seed, core, devein, and finely chop the jalapeño chile, banana pepper, and bell peppers. Chop the onion.

In a medium bowl, combine all the ingredients. Mix together well.

CORN AND ORANGE TOMATO SALSA

Chunky and brimming with vegetables, this salsa is particularly at home atop Crunchy Black Bean Cakes (page 187) and would go well with almost any of the potato chips and plantain chips in our Vegetables chapter. Diminutive and pretty orange plum tomatoes are beginning to show up in supermarket produce bins. They are sweeter and less acidic than the standard red Roma tomatoes.

MAKES ABOUT 2 CUPS
(32 TABLESPOONS)

PER TABLESPOON
Fat 0 g
Protein 0 g
Carbohydrates 2 g
Calories 10

1⅓ cups fresh corn kernels

1 teaspoon water

4 orange plum tomatoes or 2 Roma tomatoes

2 green onions

½ cup chopped fresh cilantro

¼ cup plus 2 tablespoons fresh lime juice

1 teaspoon salt

½ teaspoon ground black pepper

Combine the corn and water in a microwave-safe container, cover, and microwave on HIGH power until crisp, 1 to 2 minutes.

Chop the tomatoes. Trim the green onions to white and light green parts, and chop.

In a medium bowl, combine the corn, tomatoes, green onions, cilantro, lime juice, salt, and pepper. Mix well.

WASABI CREAM

MAKES ABOUT ¾ CUP
(12 TABLESPOONS)

PER TABLESPOON
Fat 1.5 g
Protein 1 g
Carbohydrates 1 g
Calories 25

Powerful wasabi powder, sold in Asian and gourmet markets, has a flavor very much its own. It's made from the same horse-radish-like Japanese root as the paste you mix into soy sauce for dipping sushi. Our spicy Wasabi Cream sets off Crusty Soft-Shell Crabs (page 100) or Salt Cod and Potato Cakes (page 140) nicely.

1 tablespoon plus 1 teaspoon wasabi powder

1 teaspoon fresh lemon juice

¾ cup reduced-fat sour cream

1 teaspoon sesame oil

1 tablespoon chopped green onion

1 tablespoon chopped fresh cilantro

In a small bowl, dissolve the wasabi powder in the lemon juice. Set aside at room temperature for 5 minutes, then fold in the sour cream, oil, green onion, and cilantro.

CAPER CREAM

Piquant caper sauces just seem to set off wild rice dishes, and we pair this Caper Cream with Wild Rice Pancakes (page 196) and with Wild Rice Cakes with Smoked Trout (page 194). Look for the more flavorful large capers rather than the tiny nonpareils.

1/4 cup reduced-fat mayonnaise

2 tablespoons reduced-fat sour cream

2 tablespoons finely chopped capers

2 teaspoons snipped fresh chives

Mix together the mayonnaise and sour cream in a small bowl. Stir in the capers and chives.

MAKES ABOUT 1/2 CUP
(8 TABLESPOONS)

PER TABLESPOON
Fat 1.5 g
Protein 0 g
Carbohydrates 1 g
Calories 20

HORSERADISH CREAM

MAKES ABOUT ½ CUP
(ABOUT 8 TABLESPOONS)

PER TABLESPOON
Fat 1.5 g
Protein 1 g
Carbohydrates 2 g
Calories 25

This cream is made with grated horseradish root, the stuff from which the prepared horseradish sold in bottles is made. While somewhat tamer than the Japanese horseradish root from which wasabi is derived, it is still pungent enough to provide character. We particularly like it with Spicy Shrimp Hush Puppies (page 110) and on Oyster Po'boys (page 123).

½ cup reduced-fat sour cream

1 teaspoon Dijon mustard

2 tablespoons grated horseradish root

½ teaspoon Creole seasoning (prepared or page 25)

¼ teaspoon salt

¼ teaspoon ground black pepper

Mix the sour cream and mustard together in a small bowl. Add the horseradish, Creole seasoning, salt, and pepper. Mix thoroughly.

APPLE CHUTNEY

We created this relatively mild, sweet chutney with Chive-Potato Pancakes (page 178) in mind, but it also goes quite well with Unfried Pork Chops (page 56), Pita Pocket Chips (page 188), and Apple Pancakes (page 220). Use a fairly mild variety of curry powder for this recipe.

2 medium Golden Delicious apples

¼ cup fresh lemon juice

2 tablespoons packed dark brown sugar

2 teaspoons curry powder

½ cup seedless raisins

2 teaspoons honey

2 teaspoons tarragon vinegar

Peel and dice the apples.

Combine the apples, lemon juice, brown sugar, and curry powder in a microwave-safe container. Microwave on HIGH power for 2 minutes, then stir. Microwave for 1 minute more, then stir and mash lightly, taking care to leave about half of the apple chunks intact. Stir in the raisins, honey, and vinegar.

MAKES ABOUT 1 CUP
(16 TABLESPOONS)

PER TABLESPOON
Fat 0 g
Protein 0 g
Carbohydrates 9 g
Calories 35

TOMATO BROTH

MAKES ABOUT **3 ⅓ CUPS**
(ABOUT 53 TABLESPOONS)

PER TABLESPOON
Fat 0 g
Protein 0 g
Carbohydrates 0 g
Calories 0

We call for canned diced tomatoes in this recipe because they are so readily available. If, however, your market stocks the new chopped tomatoes in a box, buy them without a second thought. Imported from Italy, the tomatoes taste wonderful, contain no additives, and have none of the metallic undertaste that can plague the canned variety. We use Tomato Broth as a sauce for Grandma's Chiles Rellenos (page 34), and drizzle it over Eggplant Panini (page 174) and Polenta Panini (page 192).

1 (14½-ounce) can diced tomatoes

1 clove garlic, chopped

¼ cup roughly chopped yellow onion

2 cups defatted chicken broth (canned or page 19)

Pinch of cayenne pepper

Combine the tomatoes, garlic, and onion in the bowl of a food processor. Pulse until almost smooth, about 12 times. Transfer the mixture to a medium nonstick skillet and cook over medium heat until it is very thick, about 10 minutes.

Stir in the broth and the cayenne. Increase the heat to medium-high, bring to a boil, and boil for 5 minutes. Skim off any foam that forms on top.

INDEX